Improve Cashflow *Thru'* Inventory Control

Shunsuke Tsuda (Japan) & Samir Kumar Manna (India)
This literature is based on a Japanese book by Toshiko Shibata

ST Associates (Japan)
Torque Management Services (India)

BLUEROSE PUBLISHERS
India | U.K.

Copyright © Mr Shunsuke Tsuda & Mr Samir Kumar Manna 2025

All rights reserved by author. No part of this publication may be reproduced, stored in a retrieval system or transmitted in any form or by any means, electronic, mechanical, photocopying, recording or otherwise, without the prior permission of the author. Although every precaution has been taken to verify the accuracy of the information contained herein, the publisher assumes no responsibility for any errors or omissions. No liability is assumed for damages that may result from the use of information contained within.

BlueRose Publishers takes no responsibility for any damages, losses, or liabilities that may arise from the use or misuse of the information, products, or services provided in this publication.

For permissions requests or inquiries regarding this publication, please contact:

BLUEROSE PUBLISHERS
www.BlueRoseONE.com
info@bluerosepublishers.com
+91 8882 898 898
+4407342408967

ISBN: 978-93-7018-160-1

Cover Design: Shubham Verma
Typesetting: Sagar

First Edition: May 2025

Preface

Let me first introduce ourselves. I am one of the translators of this book. I am a Japanese consultant promoting the productivity enhancement for manufacturing companies. My friend, Mr. Samir K. Manna is the joint translator. He is an Indian consultant. He has been providing guidance to various Indian manufacturing companies on 5S, Lean and Quality Management.

The Toyota Production System (TPS) is well known worldwide as the lean management. Moreover, the Total Productive Maintenance (TPM), one of the derivatives of TPS, is another popular system. It also pursues a similar productivity improvement drive focusing on the equipment operations. A lot of TPS / TPM consultants are visiting India on a regular basis. The basic purpose is to provide necessary guidance to various companies. They do so by imparting knowledge and helping in the adoption of these systems. Thus, companies are aiming to become globally competitive with profitable growth. But it is a reality that most companies hardly bear fruit through such initiatives. According to me, there are many factors. One of the weakest areas is the inventory management or the lack of it.

As a consultant, I have one fundamental principle during any productivity enhancement project. This has been to diagnose the warehouse at the first place. My habit has been to have a close look at the stock and storage methods of various goods. Such goods consist of works-in-progress, raw materials as well as finished goods. Many basic problems come to the surface during such an exercise. Thus, this approach has always proved to be handy to build a foundation for sustained improvement in an organization!

In TPS, "Waste of inventory" forms one of the "Seven Wastes". According to TPS, stock is a waste, and there should be efforts to reduce it as much as possible. Toyota calls any stock a "Devil" as it hides other kinds of waste under its cover. But it is a reality that most managers do not understand how to deal with it in a concrete manner. This may be because they might have a bitter experience of the stock-out. Thus, such managers often feel it appropriate to maintain a so-called safer amount of stock. As a result, there are in most cases a large amount of safety stock in every process. Thus, the inevitable effect has been swelling of the stock of all kinds.

Such a way of thinking is not limited to parts and products alone. But it also infects other things such as machines, apparatus, fixtures, and tooling. Thus, it is usual to find a vast part of the factory occupied by some of these things. This becomes a serious problem when even the management remains unaware of these. They may even lack the information about when there was use of these last time!

If a manager can notice this phenomenon, then, he or she may start necessary measures to reduce the volume of inventories. They can apply some simple logic and can reduce inventories avoiding any danger of stock-out. But a big question is how to find out such logic. Education is the key! In this respect, I found the book "Inventory control" by a Japanese researcher to be very unique and informative. It is both in its content, which is so comprehensive, and its way of presentation, which is so simple. This is why we thought of translating it into English. The basic idea was to provide much-needed support to the people across the globe. This is for the people who are working now or may like to work in the future in the productivity enhancement drive.

This book specializes in the scientific management of inventory control. There are a lot of simple and real-life examples. These would help the readers understand the underlining concepts in a very clear way. It is our strong feeling that the readers will find this book a smooth reading material. They may derive a significant competitive edge by adopting the principles and methodologies. Thereby, this may lead to successful implementation of TPS and TPM.

Shunsuke Tsuda
Co-translator
Ibaraki
Japan
29/11/24
+81-90-2559-9606

Editor's note

"Improve Cash Flow Through' Inventory Control," by Toshiko Shibata, offers a comprehensive guide to optimizing inventory management for businesses to enhance their financial health. Translated from Japanese by Shunsuke Tsuda and Samir K. Manna, this book uses simple explanations and real-world examples, such as a household refrigerator, to illustrate key concepts like understanding stock origins, associated expenses, and the impact of inventory on financial statements. It further explores various stock control methodologies, including different ordering systems and the importance of warehouse organization (5S principles), while also addressing the complexities of supply chain management and waste reduction. Ultimately, the book aims to equip readers with practical knowledge to achieve efficient inventory control, leading to improved cash flow and overall business agility.

Contents

Prologue "What is the essence of inventory?" 1

Chapter 1
The profit increases when we control the stock. 21

Chapter 2
A company should capture its stock
by the number of days. 68

Chapter 3
How should we control the amount of stock? 115

Chapter 4
Warehouse and organization that
improves the power of stock 161

Chapter 5
The warehouse and the organization
that improve the inventory power 198

Chapter 6
To reduce the stock by   the supply chain 233

Afterword 251

Prologue

"What is the essence of inventory?"

1. Significance of the existence of inventory and the effect of inventory control Inventory exists for the sake of customer.

When discussing inventory, a question comes to our mind. This is, "Why is the inventory needed?" The answer is quite simple. Inventory exists to ensure prompt service to the customer. Manufacturers, wholesalers or retailers, most of the establishments maintain inventories. But it may be possible that the provider is clear about the requirements of a given commodity. Then, it is possible to take orders from the customer even without having to maintain any stock. Thus, we can say that "Business is possible without maintaining inventory."

In any business, there is a primary rationale behind maintaining inventory. It is to meet the delivery requirements of the customers. But the supplier may develop and maintain a suitable system with its customers. In such a case, the supplier may not need to maintain inventory. Any customer would usually like to receive the commodity as soon as they place the order. Often, having some inventory helps in achieving this. But the customer may be already satisfied with some kind of system in place on the part of the supplier. It is possible that the supplier prepares the commodity and delivers it within a stipulated time. So, in such a situation, maintaining any stock becomes unnecessary.

As for the stock, "Having zero stock is the best." This is the basic spirit behind undertaking this study. The reason behind the existence of stock by a supplier organization may have become clear by now. "It is to answer customer needs." A supplier needs to deliver the commodity as soon as its customer places an order.

Let's begin with the management of "the inventory of finished products."

There are several kinds of inventory in a manufacturing organization:

a) "Inventory of the finished products" which is ready for shipping to customers;

b) "Stock of the work-in-process;" and

c) "Inventory of the parts and input materials."

In this book, the focus is on "inventory of finished products." This is unless mentioned otherwise. The reason is that an organization maintains inventory to meet the customer's expectations. It is the first important thing for the organization. The basic idea behind this is to ensure the timely delivery of the commodity to its customer.

It is necessary to understand the sales situation in the market with enough accuracy. The aim in the first place is to manage the inventory of finished goods. This information should be the starting point of "the inventory control". It helps to examine how much inventory an organization should keep for the future.

The starting point is to establish a system to manage the inventory of finished goods. Then, the details like "what product, when, and how many" become clear. Such information forms the sole basis of all other types of stocks. These are like the inventory of work-in-process and the input materials.

We can understand the mechanism of inventory control by taking the example of "a refrigerator".

It is important to form a concrete image of "what or why is the inventory?" Then, we may understand the 'inventory control' in a better way. Let me explain this using a simple example of the refrigerator. This is a very common gadget used in our homes. A refrigerator is comparable to a warehouse of a company. So, we can visualize 'stock control' in a simple and familiar manner through this example.

First of all, let's think about the role of a refrigerator. Someone may say that its primary role is to cool foodstuffs and drinks. Other may say that it is to preserve and store something for a period of time keeping the quality intact. Someone may also perceive its role to be that of providing one with any food item at any point of time. Thus, "storing foodstuffs, and to be able to have what and when is necessary" are the roles of any refrigerator.

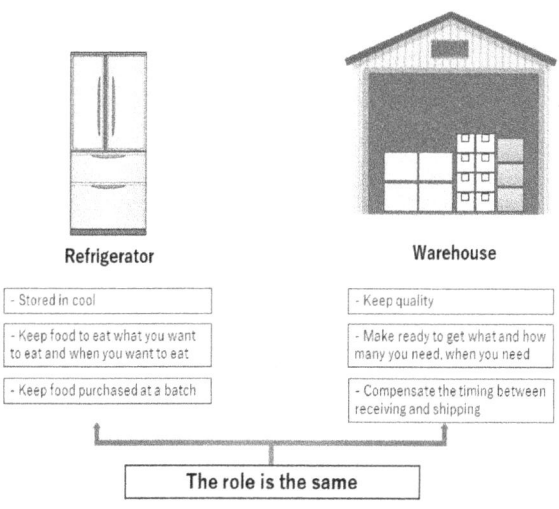

Fig. 1: Refrigerator vs. Warehouse

For instance, a person may say, "I buy a whole week's food at a time." In such a case, it becomes necessary to keep the stock in the refrigerator for the entire week. This is for the safe storage of the entire stock. Thus, a refrigerator facilitates in use of stock as per the corresponding daily requirements. The period could be according to buying frequency. It can be for a week or for a month or so. There is, thus, a gap between "Time of procurement" and "Time of consumption". We call such a gap the buffer/storage period.

We can understand roles of a refrigerator and a warehouse better from Fig. 1.

The foodstuffs stored in a refrigerator are comparable to the stock of a warehouse.

The refrigerator at our home plays the same role as the warehouse does in a company. Foodstuffs in a refrigerator are comparable to the commodities stored in a warehouse. In the case of a manufacturing company, it is usual to call the items stored in the warehouse as the products. In this book, we would like to refer any item of a wholesaler or a manufacturer as the 'commodity'.

A company keeps the commodity in the warehouse by purchasing and manufacturing it. We call such a commodity as inventory. Once there is receipt of an order for any commodity, the company ships its shipment from the warehouse. Thus, company ensures prompt delivery to the customer. The activity is quite the same as the use of a refrigerator at home. We go for shopping to buy vegetables, drinks, etc., and keep these items in the refrigerator for future use. We take out from the refrigerator what and when we need to eat and drink.

The activity of going for shopping is comparable to arranging the commodity by a company. A company either produces or buys the commodity it needs. In case of the home scenario, we go to the store and get foodstuffs and drinks by paying money. In a similar way, a company purchases the commodity by paying money to another company. Or, the company produces goods in its own factory. General practice is to store these commodities somewhere in the company. This is until there is an order from the customer. It is universal to call such commodities as the 'inventory'.

It is very important to exercise inventory control. This is so because the need for a commodity about when and of what quantity, in most cases, is unknown or unclear.

It is normal to keep stock for a while. It is like the drinks and the vegetables we store in the refrigerator at our homes. Based on what and when something we need, we take out only the necessary amount from the refrigerator. There are cases when there is no need to have any stock control. This is when it is possible to have a complete forecast of any commodity. It is about the upcoming request for 'when and what' of the commodity. In such a case, we may develop a mechanism to have such required commodities as and when we may need them. We may prepare or buy.

But it is impossible to have an accurate forecast about when and what order may come from the customer. The same holds true for the refrigerators as well. When would one feel hungry? When would one feel thirsty? What might one like to eat? Such things cannot be pre-planned. This is one of the reasons why I chose to explain 'stock control' by using the example of a refrigerator. There is a need to have stock control because we don't know about 'when and what' we may need to ship.

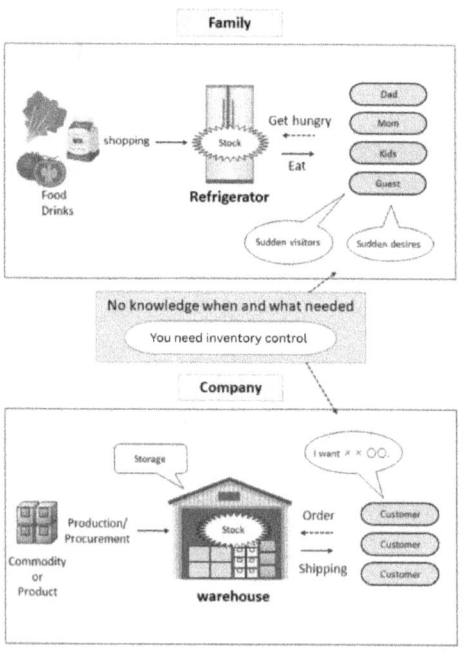

Fig. 2: Situation in a company is comparable to what happens in a family

Any failure in stock control occurs in the same way as it usually happens in the case of a refrigerator at home. Thus, we should take clues from the operation of the refrigerator at home. By this, it is possible to train ourselves in solving problems related to stock control of a company.

The effect of stock control is highly larger than we expect.

Several years ago, there was a steep hike in gasoline prices due to the oil crisis. It was quite usual to find common people rushing to gas stations around the clock. They would wait in long queues and for long hours to avail the cheapest possible deals. This was even if that meant saving as low as one yen per unit. This reflected on one's desire to support his / her household economy. This was achieved by obtaining the commodity at the cheapest possible rates.

Let us assume that one fills his / her car up to its largest capacity in the gas station. Suppose the unit price is cheaper by one yen. If the capacity of the car is 60 litre, it is possible to get the fuel at 60 yen cheaper than usual. Let's assume the average fuel consumption to be 8 km / litre. So, after full refilling, it is possible to run a distance of 480 km by the whole amount of fuel.

Say, as per normal practice, we drive 10,000 km a year as a usual "average run". This is equal to 833 km in a month. Thus, we can drive about half a month with the 60 litre of oil as mentioned above. This means that we would need about 120 litre in a month. Thus, we would be able to save an amount of 120 yen per month or 1440 yen per year.

Let's now see what happens in the case of a refrigerator. We may, at times, discard some amount of foodstuff due to various reasons. It may be due to expiry of some items, or due to excess stock of some items than required. There are situations when we may throw away some of the foodstuff. This too may be without even opening the package. Let us imagine how much one can lose through such wastage. A friend once shared a very interesting fact. She disclosed that she usually was throwing away a lot of food stuffs. It has been in the range of about 20 to 30 percent of the vegetables stored in her refrigerator per week. She was having children of growing age with good or more than average level of appetites. She has been investing a considerable amount on family's weekly food requirements. But she now realizes that she has been discarding a good amount of the food stock on a regular basis.

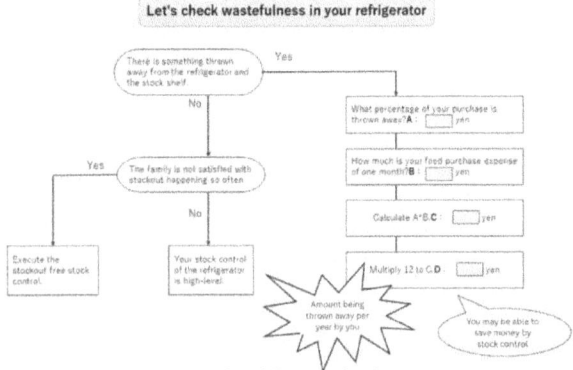

Fig. 3: A checklist to find out wastes

She shared that she was usually spending about 8,000 yen in buying foodstuffs every week. She further recalled that at least 20 percent of the stock was going to the garbage every week. This means that there was a waste of at least @1600 yen per week. Let's calculate how much cost saving is possible if we reduce this wastage by half from the existing level. It may be possible by maintaining a steady control over the stock of the refrigerator. According to a simple calculation, she has been throwing away foodstuffs of 6,400 yen monthly. Then, if she reduces such wastage by half, she can save 3,200 yen monthly. This means a saving of a considerable amount of 38,400 yen per year.

[Savings = 6,400 yen / 2 = 3,200 yen / month = 38,400 yen / year]

So, when there is 50% reduction in the quantity of vegetables thrown away, there can be an annual saving of 38,400 yen.

Now, let's understand what we can learn from the discussions on two different cases. It is quite evident where we should focus. Our aim should be to achieve most gain by putting our time, energy, and efforts. We must put in our attention to point no. 2 below which can lead to much bigger and significant savings. Outcomes expected out of the two individual cases are:

1. In the case of gasoline price hike: We could only save a meagre amount of 120 yen per month. Further, it

involves painstaking long journeys and queues.

2. In the case of excess stock in Refrigerator: There is a potential for far higher cost reduction. This is to the tune of 3,200 yen per month. Unlike in earlier case, there is no hardships and struggles involved. It only needs an effort to reduce the stock in a strategic manner. This is possible to achieve with ease by exercising necessary control over it.

We can look at the case of refrigerator from another perspective. One year consists of 52 weeks. Our friend has been discarding at least 20 % of the total food stock on an average due to various reasons. Thus, approximately 83,200 yen per year was being moved from the refrigerator to garbage (as waste). Please refer the calculation below. It is a significant amount of money. It may be more than enough for a family to spend on leisure, if saved.

[1,600 yen * 52 weeks = 83,200 yen]

It is possible to decrease the amount of food thrown away from the refrigerator to a large extent. This can be by exercising stock control of the refrigerator. The decrease of such losses can relieve the household economy to a great extent. Thus, controlling the stock of the refrigerator is far more intelligent step. It is much better than worrying about the gasoline unit price.

2. It is troublesome to have excess stock. With excess stock also we face incidences of stock outs.

The stock in a company is like cholesterol in our body.

The stock is a complex aspect of any company. On one hand, we cannot meet the customer's demand with 'zero' amount of stock. But having to deal with too much stock at a time is troublesome or risky. Let's think about if the business becomes stagnant for any reason. Then, this is likely to cause frustration for the management. This is due to the blockage of the much-needed working capital. Any company needs working capital for the regular running of its business.

When there is a lot of the stock that are stagnant, there can be other problem too apart from the cash flow problem. Company may need to buy new commodities to meet the changing requirements of the market. But there may be space constraint to store such commodities. This is so because the warehouse is already occupied with unsold products. Hence, the company would be at a constraint to avail new opportunity of making higher sales.

It is often said that "Cash is blood" for the running of any organization. Taking the analogy further, we can compare the role of inventory with that of cholesterol. Cholesterol is an indispensable nutrient for the human body. But it is detrimental to our body beyond a certain level. It blocks the blood flow, causing diseases like hypertension and arteriosclerosis. Also, there is a problem if it becomes too less. A lack of its adequate level is also harmful for the smooth functioning of the body.

We understand that it is necessary for the company to maintain some inventory in most cases. It is unless there is a mechanism in the company to ensure production without having any stock. Timely supply of the commodity as per the commitment to the customer is important. A company with too little or no stock may not function well to meet business requirements. It is like a body that may not function well due to the lack of adequate cholesterol. Thus, a company should have the stock at a suitable level. This is possible by exercising a steady control over the stock level. This way, the company can have a smooth cash flow while meeting its customer commitments.

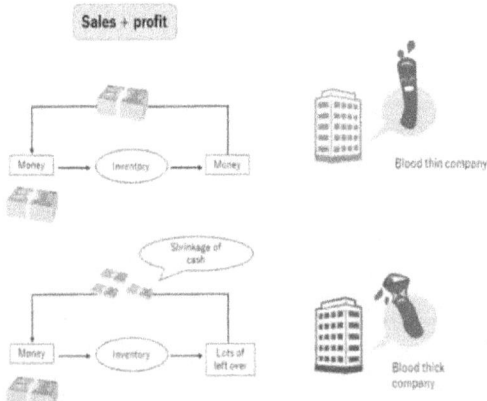

Fig. 4: Inventory is like cholesterol in the body

The 'stock' and the 'bill postponing' resemble.

Let us assume that there are two wholesalers selling the same commodity. Company A has a large amount of stock, and Company B does not have as much. In the profit ratio, company A shows a higher figure. Thus, Company A seems to be a better performer with higher profit. Now, the question is: Which of the two companies is, as a matter of fact, the better company?

To answer the question, we should have a careful look at the profit rate vis-a-vis the stock. The profit rate is the difference between the selling price and the cost of the commodities sold. Thus, the profit rate can be higher if one procures at a lower unit price by purchasing a large amount at a time. But how about the large amount of stock that remains unsold? Are we sure about the selling prospects of the commodities that remain unsold? In reality, it may be unlikely, except in a few special cases. It is interesting to note the following:

Suppose at the time of financial accounting, we do nothing about the stock of unsold stuffs. Then, we carry forward these for its disposal to the next period. We may feel the profit rate to remain intact. But there is a high probability that a pile of the unsold stock would always be sleeping in the warehouse.

The profit rate of the company falls when there is regular disposal of the unsold stock. The manager concerned generally may like to avoid any drop in the profit rate as much as possible. This is why 'disposal' is usually postponed. As a result, the task of acting upon such stock gets transferred to the next period. Or it may wait for another person to take over. This is usually called as the "Bill Postponing".

The amount of the postponed bills increases over the period of time. This is as long as the business structure doesn't change. We may be able to maintain the stock due to the availability of the necessary threshold capital. This may be a reality if there is a continuation of the regular business operations. But the capital flow might get stuck when there is a rapid depression in demand for the commodity. There may be a sudden change in the market scenario due to varied reasons. Let's consider the market situation at the time of the "Lehman Shock". To improve the flexibility of the company during such a crisis, we may avoid stock as much as possible. Stock often poses a barrier to having adequate money or cash in the system. Working capital is necessary for the smooth running of the business in the upcoming future.

In conclusion, we observe that Company B runs its business with a lesser amount of stock. Hence, it might be far steadier and healthier, even if the profit rate is lesser. Company B might continue to remain more stable than Company A, in financial terms.

	Company A	Company B
Profit rate	High	Low
Inventory	Many	Few

If the stock doesn't sell

	Company A	Company B
Storage cost	Big	Small
Disposal cost	Big	Small
Cash in hand	Little	Much
Judgement	Large potential risk	Small risk and enough cash. High flexibility for crisis

Fig. 5: Comparison of Company A vs. Company B

There is a fear of the black-ink bankruptcy too, without stock control.

There is a word, "black-ink bankruptcy". It means a wasteful phenomenon that causes the company to go bankrupt. This is even after the company has been in 'black' (i.e., profitable with positive earnings) in the business. There is a reason why such a business goes bankrupt in spite of being in the black ink. This happens due to insufficient cash in the company. But the company has to pay for the purchased goods and repay the debts taken from the bank. It is also said to be the 'failure of financing'.

Management of the company needs to fulfil the following to perform well. It should adjust itself in an efficient manner. It is about the time and amount of cash between the incoming and outgoing funds of the company. The best policy for creating such a balanced flow of cash would be to:

a) "Receive the money from the customer as early as possible, and

b) Pay the supplier as later as possible."

For this, there has to be a suitable agreement between the company and its suppliers. This is to ensure that the company doesn't suffer from 'failure of financing'. But the fact is that it may not be so simple!

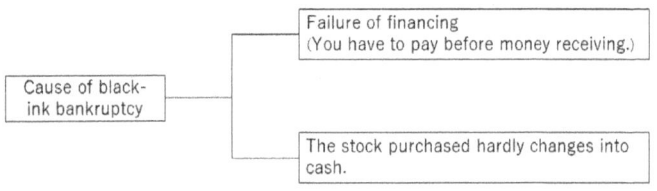

Fig. 6: Causes of black-ink bankruptcy

Furthermore, it is quite natural, "there is a general tendency that the stock swells up if we don't regulate it". Suppose we leave the stock in the warehouse for a long time. Then, it will take much more time than expected for the commodity to give returns. In the worst case, it may remain sleeping in the warehouse forever. Possibility of the "black-ink bankruptcy" may also arise under such circumstances.

Let's check our ability in stock control.

Let's understand how to improve the stock control of a

company. For this, it is important that its employees have the required abilities and skills. To have an image of the stock control ability, I have made a checklist (as shown in Table 1). This is taking a clue from the model of the refrigerator at home. We call it a 'good refrigerator' if it fulfills the following conditions:

1) The things stored consist of only the necessary ones;

2) The quality of the stored items is in a safe and hygienic state; and

3) It is convenient to take any specific item as and when it may be necessary.

This seems natural and easy. But, in reality, it is quite difficult. Let's try to check for ourselves using the checklist provided in Table 1. This is by marking points according to the real status of our own refrigerators. The full mark is 20 points. The marking scheme is:

a) A score of plus one (+1) when the response is 'applicable' in the case under consideration, and

b) Minus one (-1) if the response is 'not applicable'.

There is another table (Table 2). This provides the classification of various aspects. This forms the basis of the checkpoints listed in Table 1. Through this exercise, it would be possible to identify the weaknesses. Thus, it would also be possible to strengthen these points.

Stock control ability check seat

1. There is a door unable to open except rearranging surroundings. ☐
2. There are some doors and drawings locked out. ☐
3. The contents are too much to control. ☐
4. There are some vegetables unknown when purchased. ☐
5. The things thought to have eaten up or being forgotten are often found. ☐
6. You often forget to buy necessary things. ☐
7. There are some uncertain contents in it though moves to a container. ☐
8. You often forget the content you ordered by the mail order or web service. ☐
9. You buy inadvertently commodities on sale. ☐
10. A lot of leftovers are being kept in the refrigerator. ☐
11. There are lots of vegetables too good to throw away but no mind to use. ☐
12. The things bulk-bought cheaply remain long in the refrigerator. ☐
13. There are some unable to abandon though out of validity in the fridge. ☐
14. There are some unable to feel like eating due to the taste though in the valid period. ☐
15. It collapses unless taking out very carefully. ☐
16. It collapses even though you think piled up beautifully. ☐
17. You are often hard to find what you are sure. ☐
18. Some sauce is leaking from the container and making surroundings dirty. ☐
19. You don't have a knowledge about the meal schedule of other members in the family. ☐
20. When you bought a new article, a family member bought the same thing. ☐

【Marking】

0～9 Points	➡	Beginner
10～14 Points	➡	Average
15～20 Points	➡	Proficient

Table 1: A self-help checklist to monitor efficiency of use of a refrigerator

Aspect of stock control ability	Related items in Table 1
Is not the property wasted?	1, 2
Are the amount and the content of the stocks under control?	3, 4, 5, 6, 7
Are the amount and the content of purchase under control?	8, 9
Are the amount and the content of consumption under control?	10, 11
Well sorted?	12, 13, 14
Well put into order?	15, 16, 17
Well cleaned?	18
Enough communication between parties?	19, 20

Table 2: A typical list of various aspects of a refrigerator

Lessons the translators have got from Prologue:

1. Inventory is necessary. But too much of it may lead a company to the difficulty. It acts in the same way as cholesterol in the blood of our body.

2. Managers of a company should have the ability of stock control. They must recognize that they can avoid the black-ink-bankruptcy.

Chapter 1

The profit increases when we control the stock.

1. What is the purpose of having stock?

Stock helps in making a prompt response to the customer's request.

We should have a clear understanding of why inventory exists for. For this, let's think about a method of working with zero stock. This is as an apotheosis that would lead to the drastic reduction of the stock. It is the sales department in a company that needs inventory to serve its customers.

Let's try to have a rough understanding of the flow of the needs of the sales operation. It is a flow that starts from promotion to the sale of a commodity through different stages. These are like receiving the order, delivering the product, and completing the sales. It is quite easy to understand that there is a need for inventory in the stage of delivering the commodity. It is not necessary before that stage. But one may think that it is necessary even in the stage of receiving the order. This is why there is a need to check if the commodity is available in the inventory. By this, a company verifies the possibility of keeping its promise with the customer. But, as a matter of fact, inventory is not necessary at this stage in every circumstance. There are situations when the operation with zero stock is possible. This means that the company manufactures the product after receiving the order. It is true as long as the company can keep the due date with its customer. There may be another case. In this, it takes a longer time to manufacture the product after receiving the order. Thus, it may be difficult to meet customer commitment. In such a case, a company needs to maintain the inventory.

The inventory is to fill the gap.

Suppose, a customer places an order on a company for certain quantity of a commodity with a specified delivery period. The company may be in a position to prepare or buy only a part of the quantity required during the same period. We call the difference between these two quantities as the gap.

For instance, let us assume that the production volume of ice cream in a certain factory is 10,000 pieces per month. This company knows from experience that there are fluctuations in the sales volume. This variation is seasonal. Sales volume reaches up to 30,000 pieces per month at midsummer. So, there would be a gap of 20,000 pieces in production and the sales volume during this season.

If the company tries to produce the whole volume during midsummer, it will fall short by 20,000 pieces. In such a case, the company advances the production timing. The basic idea behind this is to build the stock to correspond to the selling timing of the ice cream.

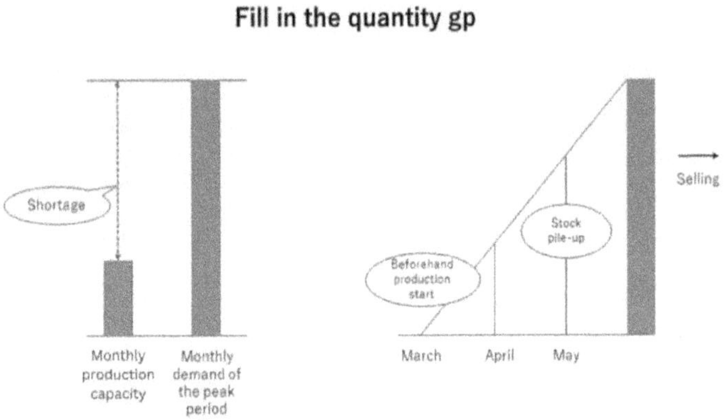

Fill in the quantity gp

Fig 7: Building stock to meet seasonal high sales requirements

There are some commodities that are usually sold throughout the year. It is possible that there are consistent and regular requirements. But there may be a constraint by way of a limited production periods. A commodity like rice is a simple example. We buy and eat rice throughout the year. But the harvesting time is only the summer and the autumn.

In such a case, there is a large gap in time periods between production and consumption. To take care of this, the option available is to manage by keeping the inventory corresponding to the gap. So, it is usual to produce such commodities in excess by planning and maintaining adequate stock. The idea is to sell it in the market at all the time throughout the year or, in other words, at the time there is a need.

Fill in the timing gap

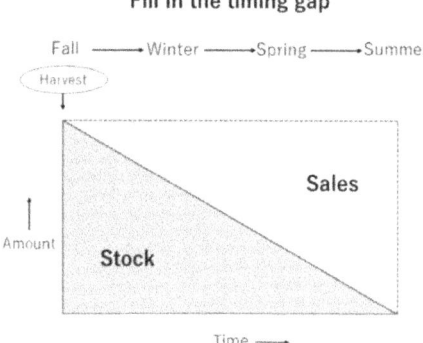

Fig.8: Building stock to take care of seasonal production

2. Why does the stock rise?

Stock rises due to the functioning style of production and purchasing divisions.

A company prepares a stock of some commodities for sale by producing and purchasing. Manufacturing and Purchasing divisions are the ones that give birth to inventory. But there may be other reasons too that lead to the building of some undesirable stock. A company may decide to produce and buy some commodities at cheap rates in the hope of future sales. Moreover, there is another interesting thing that causes inventory build-up too. This is due to the style of performance evaluation of the staff of production and purchasing. Such appraisals may include criteria like the unit cost of production and procurement. So, it becomes quite important to adopt a strategy of keeping the unit cost of the commodity as low as possible. Thus, the focus of the staff working gets shifted. They try to achieve a good rating during the process of such management appraisals. They do so by producing or buying commodities in bulk to secure lower costs! As a result, it becomes a natural practice to produce and buy in larger quantities. These commodities, then, get transferred to the warehouse as stock at a time. Thus, this kind of management system causes a sudden sharp rise in the inventory.

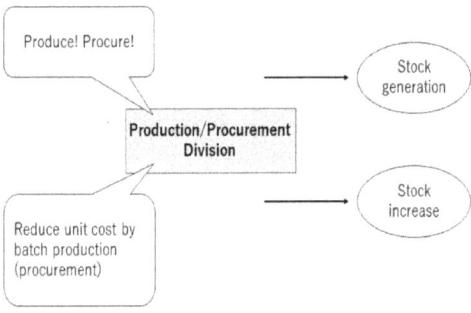

Fig. 9: Rise of inventory due to batch Production / Procurement

The stock also rises due to the activity of the sales department.

Sales department of a company is at a critical juncture in any business. The sales staffs need to maintain a direct communication with the customer. Thus, they act in such a way that they can fulfil the customer's request without fail.

Furthermore, any sales staff is also usually evaluated in a particular manner. This is by the volume of sales executed through him or her in most companies. So, he or she tries their best to avoid the situation of stock-out of any commodity for which there may be an order. He or she is always interested to fulfil the order of any commodity without fail. Thus, there is a tendency to keep a lot of stock to avoid any situation of 'stock out'. Often, there are Production and Procurement divisions that prepare the commodity. These departments work on building stocks as per needs of the sales department. The sales department tends to put up higher demand such that there would never be any 'stock out'. In most cases, the sales department is strong enough to force other divisions to meet the request.

Thus, the sales department is also responsible for a higher level of the inventory in a company. It does so by raising strong demand to avoid missing out any potential sales due to 'stock out'. Sales staffs often work with a sole aim to show up better during the performance evaluation by the management.

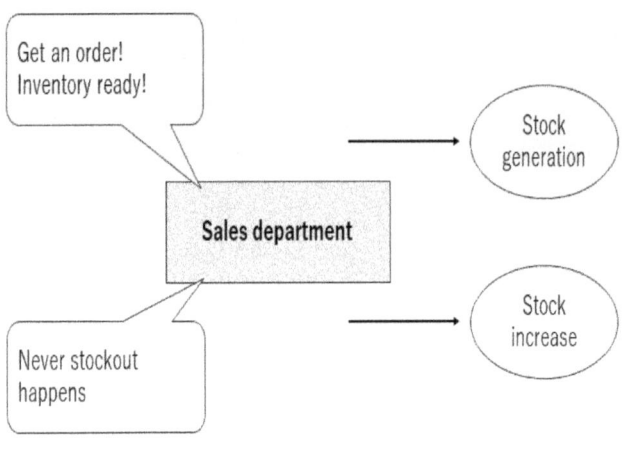

Fig. 10: Rise of inventory caused by the working of the Sales Division

The logistics division doesn't give birth to the stock.

We may think the logistics division has a deep connection in the build-up of the inventory. But, as a matter of fact, it doesn't generate any stock at its own. Sometimes, the logistics division may seem to prepare some stock. But we cannot consider this as a result of the own activity of the logistics division. They usually do so according to the instructions of the sales department. Hence, we cannot conclude that the logistics division builds such stocks.

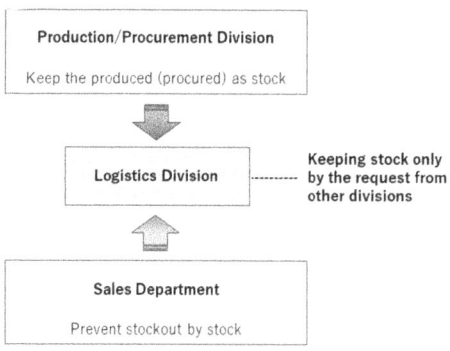

Fig. 11: Logistics Division under the influence of Production / Procurement and Sales Divisions

The logistics division stores the commodities that the production division produces. Also, the logistics division keeps commodities that belong to the sales division. The sales division secures such stock from the production division. So, the logistics division does the mere function of storage for other divisions. There is a deeper relation between the stock and these three divisions. So, 'how to manage the stock' in such a situation is a very crucial matter.

3. What kinds of expenses are there in maintaining the inventory?

Cost to secure the stock.

It costs to have the stock. It is quite easy to imagine about the production and buying costs. But actually, there are a lot of other costs too. Let's begin with the cost to secure the stock. Let me call both "Production" and "Buying" as "Procurement" for this discussion.

We may be quite conversant about the operation of a convenience store. A clerk feeds the input data to the terminal of a computer. For this, he or she makes manual checking of the quantity of the commodities lying on the shelves of the store. The method of procuring stock is by ordering. Thus, there are the following typical expenses:

a) Personnel expenses. This is to take care of ordering and feeding data on receipt of goods and during other transactions.

b) Expenses to have the computer terminal, communication network, and related accessories; and

c) In some companies, there are periodic meetings. This is to examine and decide what and how many commodities to order. The personnel expense of the attendees of such meetings also adds to the cost of ordering.

Now, it is quite easy to understand that one of the major costs is the 'personnel cost'. In general, we may not be worrying about this, considering the personnel expense is a fixed cost. But we can reduce such cost by shortening the order processing time. This is especially in the case when there is overtime working in ordering. There may also be a sacrifice of other works due to the time consumed in the ordering operation.

The cost of the inventory itself

"The cost of the inventory" is the price to pay a) as a commodity fee to the supplier or b) as the cost of production. We should not forget about this cost. We often tend to get any commodity in bulk quantity at the cheapest possible rates. The thinking behind it is that this would lead to an increase in the profit. But we should also know that this condition would hold true only under a certain condition. The condition is when it is possible to sell all the commodities procured. We may also succeed in reducing the unit cost by mass production. But it may cost far more when a large amount of goods remains unsold.

Cost of the stock keeping

Adequate storage space is necessary for maintaining the stock. The costs of the warehouse include:

a) warehouse rent (or owning a warehouse, applicable taxes etc.),

b) insurance,

c) utility, and

d) labour of the warehouse operation as well as its management.

There may be extra costs towards having:

a) a suitable 'stock control information system',

b) material handling and storage aids such as racks, forklifts, and trolleys, etc.

Once we have the space necessary to keep goods, we may consider it as a natural expense. This may be due to it being a part of the fixed costs and thus, there may be hardly any interest in reducing this cost. Yet, it is necessary to examine the warehouse on a regular basis and in a purposeful way. We may enquire like: "Is the present size necessary? Is the warehouse in that particular place a must?" etc.

There are cases when the space for the stock may be expanding even before we realize it. This usually happens because of:

a) increase in volume of the dealing commodities,

b) hike in business scope, and

c) bulk-buying for reduction of unit cost.

Moreover, with a lot of stocks, we may have to give priority to the more effective use of the space. As a result, the operational efficiency might become worse. There may be occasions when we can't put goods on the shelves. Then, we may put some commodities directly on the ground blocking the passages or gangways This may cause disturbance in the regular working of the warehouse. Hence, the operational efficiency would decrease. This may lead to extra time working. This means increased cost of operation due to the need for overtime payment.

It is quite cynical that the stock obstructs the business. But it actually happens so often. If we have a lot of stock, we may have to have a wider space for it, and that may be at times more than necessary. This can also be a significant factor that may reduce the operational efficiency. We must understand the speed of reaching out to a necessary commodity. It differs a lot between strolling through a wider space and picking the same from a narrower space. In other words, it is far easier and quicker to find a necessary commodity from a space that is not very wide! To exercise control for containing the stock is very important. This is with a view to bring down the expense of the 'stock keeping'.

Interest rate costs the stock keeping.

There is another cost too. It is common to call this as the "Interest cost". We need money to have inventory for carrying out production and purchasing. When we buy the stock by taking the loan from the bank, it costs us interest. This is also a part of the cost of stock keeping. If we buy an extra amount of stock, the debt on account of this amount might be quite high. It is very obvious that this would result into an extra cost towards the interest. But any reduction in the stock would lead to a commensurate reduction in the cost of stock keeping.

There are risks associated with the stock keeping.

Suppose we keep the stock for a long time. Then, there are certain risks involved. For instance, the stock might get damaged in the warehouse over the period of time. Also, there might be deterioration in the quality of the goods. It is natural that we cannot sell any deteriorated goods. So, all the costs invested in such stocks would then become a waste.

Moreover, there is another possible risk. Value of the stocked commodity may fall due to a change in popularity. So, its price may go down under such circumstances. Profit would decrease in such a case even if there are some sales. Thus, the cost of maintaining the stock would further go up. The worst situation we may face is when we cannot sell the commodity at all, even by cutting down the price. In such a situation, there may be no other way but to dispose-off the stock. This will lead the company to incur extra costs at the end. Please read the following paragraph for better understanding.

The cost to abandon the stock is quite high.

It is the cost to abandon the unsalable stocks. We should avoid this as most of the costs related to such stocks go to waste. There is another aspect. If there is a generation of any abandonment cost, it may reflect a "Tip of the iceberg of wasteful costs". It may be like finding out "A big goldmine". The reason for this is the following:

Abandonment cost of unsaleable stocks has many components. It includes all the costs of examination, procurement, inventory management for the commodity. All these cost components become wasteful because of 'no possibility of sale'.

The abandoned stock is a kind of stock we could have avoided to prepare at all from the very beginning. This is possible if we can have accurate judgement whether the stock is necessary or not. Such assessment would help in containing the 'cost of abandonment' to the lowest level.

4. What would happen if we do not manage the stock?

The goal of the stock control is not about controlling the Quality. It is about control of the Quantity of the stock.

The aim of controlling the stock is to control the quantity of the stock. There is also another meaning of the stock control. It means to manage 'How to keep the quality of the stock'. But in this book, I limit the meaning of the 'stock control' to controlling the 'quantity of the stock'.

It is important to control the quality of the commodity in the warehouse. But, as discussed in the earlier clause, if a commodity is not sold finally, its stock doesn't have any meaning. Thus, quality control of it using extra cost doesn't have any meaning either. In other words, the cost that we may incur for quality control measures would also become a waste!

First of all, we have to control the quantity of stock. This is to avoid paying for a lot of meaningless costs. These are like the cost of:

a) abandonment, and

b) extra work by making workers perform any unnecessary job.

It is quite usual to encounter the state of overstock and 'stock out' at the same time.

Improper management of the stock causes the 'stock out' and the overstock at the same time. The 'stock out' is a state when there is missing of an order due to 'no stock'. It means non-availability of the stock of the required commodity. A company loses sales in such circumstances. The company often considers it as a big loss. 'Overstock' means to have more than the necessary amount of stock. There are cases when we do not recognize that there is an existence of overstock of a commodity. This is because in most cases, companies do not understand the right amount of stock they should keep.

The 'stock out' is easier to find out. But if there is stock out of any commodity, there would be a case of overstock as well. This is quite interesting! Any incidence of the 'stock out' indicates that there is a lack of inventory control. Inventory control is about maintaining the appropriate quantities of the stocks.

There may be several warehouses in a company situated at different locations. There may be different situations of "stock out" and "overstock" in each of the warehouses. For example, it is possible that there is excess stock of commodity 'X' in 'B' warehouse. At the same time, there may be a 'stock out' of the same in 'A' warehouse. We call such an unevenness of the stock as "Uneven distribution of the stock". It is possible to reduce amount of excess stock in 'B' warehouse by transferring it to 'A' warehouse. Also, by this, it is possible to overcome the problem of the stock-out of 'A' warehouse. But the usual pattern of inventory management we often find is quite different. There may be an urgent procurement of commodity 'X' for 'A' warehouse. It is usual that the company forgets to make use of the excess stock of the same lying in 'B' warehouse. So, we should manage the quantity of the stock from the viewpoint of the whole company. Otherwise, we cannot avoid such a waste.

Amount of 'long-term stock' rises in the absence of stock control.

If we neglect stock control, there is every possibility of some serious problems. There may be generation of a kind of stock that might be in the warehouse for a long time. We call this phenomenon as aging of the stock. Also, it may go almost unnoticed by the warehouse management personnel. I mentioned here a term, "almost unnoticed". This means that a part of the stock might remain long time without shipment as expected. In real life scenarios, we may often find such stocks that might be lying for more than several years. There are several names of such stocks. The names are like "Long-term stock", "Non-moving stock", and "Stay or dead stock", etc.

About such 'non-moving stock', we often adopt a typical approach. We continue to keep the stock considering that we would be able to sell these sooner or later. But actually, it is very rare that a commodity, whose sale has once gone down, can ever improve again. So, the question arises if we should keep on maintaining such commodities in stock or not. What should we do if we have the commodities in stock that are lying for a long time? There may not be sale of such commodities in the future. So, it is best to dispose these off when any stagnation comes to notice. This way, there can be far lesser cost in the stock keeping. We have to face a regrettable situation otherwise. After spending a lot of time and cost, the commodities may become a total waste or scrap.

So, it is of immense importance that we control the quantity of the stock with utmost care. This is to avoid the generation of such 'stay stock'.

Nobody leaves the vegetable in the refrigerator for a

long time.

It is not unusual to have some stock for a long time in a warehouse. This is unless a company has a careful management of stocks of various commodities. Non-moving stock would exist as a natural fall-out if there is no system of inventory control. The important question now in our mind may be: "Why does a company keep stock of such commodities that is improbable to sell in near future?"

In case of storing the vegetable in the refrigerator, there is an advantage. The time when we can't use a particular foodstuff any longer is quite easy to visualize. For instance, there can be some visible symptoms of such a situation. This may be in the form of some physical changes. For example, "shrivel" occurs due to loss of moisture in vegetables. Nobody might leave the shriveled greens for a long time, once discovered. In short, if we can notice stagnation of any stock, we would be able to deal with it. If there is any stagnated stock, one would use it anyway at the first possible opportunity. It is one of the secrets of keeping the stock afresh always.

There is something like the shriveled vegetable in the warehouse of a company, too. It is "a kind of commodity that was not having much shipping recently." Such commodities might have been in the category of marketable goods till some time ago. It is natural to have rotations of the commodities in a warehouse i.e. it come in and go out. Suppose we leave a commodity as it is which has not been getting shipped of late. Then, we may face problem of shipping of such commodity in near future. When we leave such non-moving goods as it is, it stays in the warehouse. It works like a pest. It occupies the valuable storage space in the warehouse. So, there has to have a system for prompt identification of such commodities in any warehouse. One must put regular focus on items that have been showing a clear pattern of decrease in the pace of shipment. On the basis of such observations, there has to be appropriate countermeasures. Idea is that a company should take such actions before there is a complete stop of sales. The discounted sale often becomes one of the measures to mitigate such circumstances. We call such a sale as 'bargain' sale also.

It is very important not to miss any such symptom of adverse change in sales pattern. This can be by continuous monitoring of status of the warehouse by use of data. Otherwise, it would be difficult to gauge any perceptible change. This is like the case of storage of vegetables in the refrigerator. I am going to explain later in this chapter about how to check the situation using data.

5. How does the stock influence the financial statement?

Financial statements are the health reports of a company.

What could be the management situation of the company if the stock control is not adequate? There are various kinds of "Financial statements" in a company. Its purpose is to have an appropriate assessment of company's management situation. Thus, we may consider these statements as the 'health reports' of the company. From such statements, it is possible to understand if the company is going well or not.

"Money is like blood for a company." The stock of a company is comparable to "Cholesterol" of a human body. Cholesterol is necessary and indispensable to keep the human body healthy and strong. But excess of it beyond a limit might get accumulated inside the passage of blood vessel. It might cause contraction of the passage. Thus, it might disturb smooth flow of blood through it. Also, excess cholesterol might get oxidized and become nothing but a 'waste matter'. Excess inventory has a similar effect in the performance of a company. It might impede the flow of much needed cash. Thus, it may hamper smooth running of the business and can cause poor health condition of the company.

"Stock" appears in the balance sheet.

Let's see how the health report of the company pays attention to the stock. There are three kinds of financial statement. These are: a) the Balance Sheet, b) the Statement of Income (or of Profit and Loss) and c) the Statement of Cash Flow. The balance sheet shows the following:

a) how the company procures the capital for the business, and

b) what kind of asset the company has.

Balance sheet

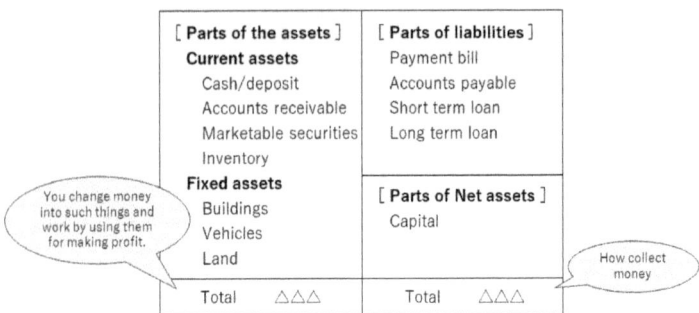

Fig. 12: Elements of Balance Sheet

It serves as a statement of the financial position of a company. In it, there are assets in one section (left side) and liabilities and net worth in the other section (right side). In this statement, there is an exact "balance" between these two sections. The right side of the balance sheet shows the methods that has been used to get funds. There are several means of such funding:

a) Taking loan from bank,

b) Collecting capital from shareholders, and

c) Putting in profit the company has earned.

It is a convention to mention the debt (i.e., the liabilities) and the net assets in the right side of the statement.

A company spends cash for acquiring various assets. The left side of the balance sheet records this plus the balance cash that remains in hand. The company might use money to buy fixed assets. These are like building, equipment and the investment trust. The assets are of two types: a) the current assets and b) the fixed assets. This depends upon how easy to liquidate the cash.

There is an underlining principle in making a Balance sheet. The right side and the left side of this table should tally exactly every time. This is in monetary term. Inventory is an essential input in the balance sheet. Let's try to find out which part of the balance sheet includes this. As per prevailing norm, "inventory" is a part of the current assets. A company usually maintains inventory by using the money out of the sources like:

a) Loan from a bank,

b) Raising funds from shareholders, and /or

c) Drawing cash from the internal reserves.

Any long 'stay stock' is to appropriate as an appraisal loss!

The current assets mean such assets that a company can convert into cash within one year. My concern is whether the so-called current assets are current or not in the true sense. Suppose there are some stocks sleeping for several years in the warehouse. Then, we cannot consider that the company can convert these assets into cash within one year.

There is another aspect in the calculation too. It is whether:

a) The calculation is on the basis of the present value of such commodities, or

b) The statement is on the basis of keeping the value of the commodities the same as their initial value.

Thus, there might be room for improvement in the balance sheet of a company. This is so if there are stocks for several years and the statement is as per the original value of the commodities. If the current price is low, it makes right sense to calculate such commodities in a different way. It should be as per the current prevailing value that is lower than the original value. The company should appropriate such devaluation as an appraisal loss. In such a situation, it may be better to consult with a licensed tax accountant for some useful tax savings!

Let's see the business situation in the "Profit and Loss" statement.

The profit and loss or the income statement shows whether a company makes profit or not. The company prepares such a statement for a specific period of time. This may be for a quarter or a year or so. The company can understand from this report how much it has gained against the expenses made.

The sales amount minus the expenses made for the various inputs is the 'gross profit'. Expenses are the costs incurred for procurement of inputs of the commodities sold. There is another expense that we call "Selling and General Administrative" expense. When we deduct it from 'gross profit', we get the 'operating profit'. The "Selling and General Administrative" costs include:

a) The cost of logistics, and

b) The inventory carrying costs.

In more specific terms, these are the costs to store and transfer the stock, including:

a) Rental of the warehouse,

b) Labour cost of the personnel working in the warehouse, and

c) Cost of transportation used for the delivery of the goods and commodities.

If the stock increases, then, these costs would also show a tendency to increase. In short, having plenty of stock is a significant factor. It results in the decrease of 'operating profit' of a company.

The profit & loss statement

	Sales amount	10,000
(−)	Cost of sales	5,000
	Gross profit on sales	5,000
(−)	Selling & administrative expense	4,000
	Operating income	1,000
(+)	Non-operating income	300
(−)	Non-operating expense	500
	Ordinary income	800
	⋮	

Fig. 13: A typical statement of Profit and Loss account

Statement of cash flow can prevent the black ink bankruptcy.

The third financial statement is the statement of cash flow. It measures how well a company generates cash for the following:

a) To pay its debt obligations,

b) To fund its operating expenses, and

c) To fund any need of investments.

In other words, it shows:

a) The amount of cash expenses on various accounts, and

b) How much cash company has earned as revenues.

Such statement is as a standard practice for a certain period of time such as a quarter or a financial year or so.

Cash flow statement

Cash flow of operation
  Net income before tax
  Depreciation
  (+) (−) Inventory
    ⋮

Cash flow of Investment

Cash flow of Finance

Fig. 14: Cash Flow classifications

It might be the most important of all the financial statements to assess if the company is healthy. It is a must for all the listed companies to make a statement of cash flow. But even small and medium-sized companies should be more careful about their cash flow.

I have introduced the word "Black-ink bankruptcy" in the Prologue section of this book. A company may have a lot of surpluses on books according to the profit and loss statement. Yet it may fail to meet the financing requirements of the company. In such a state, we call the company has gone into bankruptcy. This is a tragedy that occurs when the cash flow is not managed well in a company.

Accumulation of the stock deteriorates the circulation of cash in a company.

Let's see the relation between cash flow and stock. Stock is a commodity that a company purchases by using cash. In other words, it is one aspect that influences to a significant extent on the 'cash in hand' status of a company. It has potential to change the financial health of a company as it impedes the cash flow.

Any company should have the freedom to use cash for anything. But there is a big problem if a bulk of its cash gets transferred into the stock. Then, the money gets blocked. The company would have to wait until there is unlocking of such cash through regular sales of the stock.

If a company can sell its non-moving stock, the revised statement of profit and loss will reflect this. Such sales are often as a result of the liquidation efforts of the company. But the company may not feel any immediate relief in the cash flow. The reason for this is that the actual payment might be pending and it might come later. Thus, the company may still face a critical situation in the cash flow. This is particularly so if a large payment liability comes before receipt of the cash.

Judging from the financial health point of view, it is not at all good to have stocks beyond a certain level. A company where there is a lot of stocks may face the problem of stagnation in the cash flow. This happens when the quantity of the stocks is far more than the necessity. It may so happen that the company cannot run its business in a smooth manner due to the cash crunch. It is comparable to the blood flow in the human body. It cannot counter heavy accumulation of cholesterol inside the blood vessels. Such a situation would hamper the smooth circulation of blood. Thus, this would lead to improper performance of the human body.

6. Inventory obstructs the health of an enterprise.

We cannot judge the financial health situation of a company only by the profit rate.

Let's analyse the management situation, paying attention to the following case.

There were three independent wholesalers in a city dealing in the same commodity. All have been maintaining some inventory. Table in Fig. 15 shows a summary of the necessary data related to the topic I am discussing. I have taken out these data from the financial statements of these three companies.

To keep the matter simple, say, every wholesaler was having 10 million yen in the beginning. With this amount of cash in hand, they decided to do the business on the same commodity. Both wholesaler A and wholesaler B purchased 100 numbers of commodities each. The buying price was 10,000 yen a piece. So, they used 1 million yen each for the buying. Wholesaler C purchased 1,000 numbers of commodities by using 9.5 million yen. Due to bulk buying, the wholesaler C could bargain a special discount. The buying price in this case was lower at 9,500 yen a piece. Suppose the selling price of this commodity was 20,000 yen in the market. "Selling and General Administration" expense is 5000 yen per unit. Let's also consider that the sales condition was the same for all three wholesalers. In such a case, the wholesaler C seems to be in a good management grade. This is because this wholesaler having advantage of a lower unit price in buying. One year passed by, and the closing accounts situation of each wholesaler was as follows:

Wholesaler A sold out all the 100 numbers of commodities purchased. Wholesaler B sold 50 pieces of commodities and 50 pieces have remained as 'unsold'. Wholesaler C sold 100 pieces of commodities and 900 pieces have remained as 'unsold'.

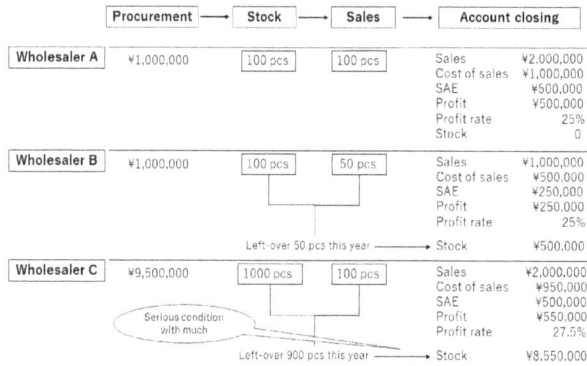

Fig. 15: A comparative Financial Statement of three Wholesalers

The stock becomes the inventory, and a company carries forward it to the next period.

Wholesaler A has sold out 100 pieces of commodities. So, his sale is 2 million yen by selling at the unit price of 20,000 yen. The "Selling and General Administration" expense is 500,000 yen @ 5000-yen cost per piece. We had the same calculation for wholesaler B and Wholesaler C, too as shown in the Table.

Well, let us compare Wholesaler A and Wholesaler B in the rows indicating the "Cost of sales". The sales figure of Wholesaler B is a half that of Wholesaler A. But the unit cost of buying was the same. Let me call the "Cost of sales" as the 'sales cost' hereafter. Calculation is on basis of the quantity sold only. For Wholesaler A, sales cost is for all 100 pieces of commodities purchased. But for Wholesaler B, sales cost is only for the 50 pieces of commodities he could sell. We calculate the operating profit by deducting the sales cost and SAE from the sales amount. SAE means the Selling and General Administration Expense.

Operating profit = sales amount - sales cost - SAE

In any business, the operating profit rate indicates a company's business performance. As per this, we would consider Wholesaler C as the best performer. We can find from the Table the following:

a) Wholesaler C has earned an operating profit of 27.5%, and

b) Both Wholesaler A and B have earned an operating profit of 25% each.

Now, let's look at the rows indicating inventory or stock in the Table. In the case of Wholesaler A, the inventory is 0 (zero) because there are no unsold commodities. In the case of Wholesaler B, 500,000 yen of the purchased cost remained unsold. This amount now remained as stock or inventory. Wholesaler C had purchased 1,000 numbers of commodities. But it could sell only 100 pieces. Thus, 900 pieces remained unsold. In this case, the unit cost of buying was 9,500 yen. Since the unsold commodities are 900 pieces, the amount of inventory becomes 8.55 million yen. This company has a big inventory. Now, there is a fear in this case!

It may have to pay a price for it in the coming future due to a huge amount of cash locked in the form of stock!

Inventory = stock, and this is nothing but locked-in cash.

Let's see the relation between the inventory and the cash flow. Wholesaler A uses 1 million yen from 10 million yen and gains 2 million yen by sales. So, and the cash flow is 11 million yen. It is desirable for the company that there is an increase in the usable cash. This is the case here. But the inventory of this wholesaler A is zero (0).

Wholesaler B uses 1 million yen from 10 million yen and gains 1 million yen by sales. Thus, there is no change in the cash flow. It remains at 10 million yen. But the inventory is 500,000 yen.

Wholesaler C uses 9.5 million yen from 10 million yen and gains 2 million yen by sales. In this case, the cash flow is minus (-) 7.5 million yen. The inventory is as big as 8.55 million yen. It is quite easy to understand that there is transformation of cash into the inventory. Now, Wholesaler C may be in a high-risk zone. The big concern is if there would be continuous sale of such a large number of commodities in the inventory! This is so because the cash is shrinking. If the consumer's preference changes, sale of the commodity would fall, as a matter of fact. It may be very difficult for Wholesaler C to sell out 8.55 million yen's worth of stock and collect cash.

Excess—amount of stock is comparable to thicker blood!

From the above discussion, one thing is very clear. The management situation of wholesaler C is not at all good. Its profit rate is found to have a better figure in the book than other companies. This is when we compare the profit and loss statements. But it is evident from the balance sheet that wholesaler C has a different picture. Most of the cash is in the locked-up state due to a large amount of inventory. According to the cash flow statement, it has used most of the cash for procurement of the stock. At the same time, its collection out of the sells is very less. It is so because a large number of products still remained as 'unsold'. The following analogy may be very useful to understand the concept better.

The stock is like 'cholesterol' in the human body. It gets accumulated inside the blood vessels when it is there in excess quantity. As a result, blood becomes thick, making it difficult to have a smooth flow. Unless there is an immediate measure, the person concerned will get sick. Cash flow is exactly like the 'flow of blood'! It may not be easy for the cash to 'come in' due to holding excess stocks. This may, in turn, hamper the smooth functioning of the business. Any organization with such a feature would finally become sick sooner or later.

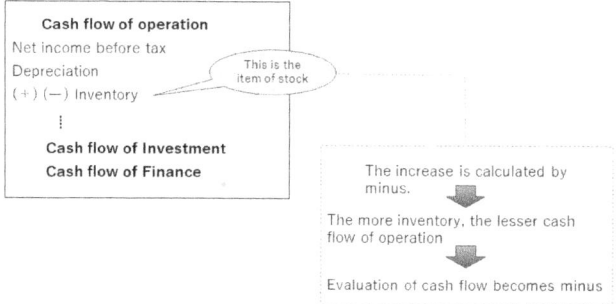

Fig. 16: Impact of inventory over cash flow

7. Appropriate stock control makes a company light and agile to any change. (with lesser burden or liability)

The balance sheet improves by proper inventory management.

By going for proper inventory management, a company becomes lighter. This is due to reduced holding of cash. Also, quick response to any change becomes possible. As a result, any company becomes much stronger with the ability to take risk. Now, we will see how an appropriate inventory management impacts the financial statements. I have picked up everything as a possibility. But I have included the extreme one.

Let's begin with observing the change in the balance sheet. It is easy to understand that it is always better to decrease accounts payable and the debt. But there are also people who don't consider it better to decrease the inventory and the fixed assets.

Inventory control can improve R.O.A.

There is an index called as R.O.A (i.e., Return on Assets). It is what the investors usually pay attention to, when they examine the worthiness to invest. This is because by going through such a parameter, they are able to see the ability of the company to make a profit. A good value of this index of the company indicates good health of the company. Investors may gather a feeling that company is earning higher profit with lesser resources. Thus, they expect such a desirable trend in the future also. We calculate R.O.A as follows:

R.O.A = [Profit / Total Capital Employed (i.e., Total Assets)] * 100

A company that may be asking its investors to buy as many stocks as possible. For this, the company has to ensure a good value of R.O.A as the first step. Now the question is: How should a company achieve a good value of R.O.A at the end? From the above-mentioned formula for calculating R.O.A, it is clear that we can have a good value of it:

a) by increasing profit, or

b) by employing lesser total capital (total assets) for doing the business, or,

c) by doing both.

So, the stock or inventory could play a significant role. If there is least possible stock, it would lead to decrease in the fixed assets, too. So, it is clear that any decrease in inventory is desirable and would lead to the improvement of R.O.A.

Working on inventory management would become exciting if we can visualize the effects. Please refer Fig. 17 for this.

Variation of Balance Sheet

Items	Improvement	Reason
Inventory	Can be reduced	Dead stock decreases
Fixed assets	Can be reduced	The area and the equipment in the warehouse can decrease due to the decrease of the stock.
Accounts payable	Can be reduced	It comes to be able to turn with a little stock.
Loan	Can be reduced	It comes to be able to turn with a little stock.
Capital adequacy rate	Can increase	The debts of accounts payable and the loan, etc. are decreased

Fig. 17: Factors influencing Balance Sheet

The capital adequacy ratio in the table is another important index. We calculate this index as per the following formula:

The capital adequacy ratio (%) =

[Capital (Free or unlocked) / Total Capital (Total Assets)] * 100

In financial terms, a company is healthier if it has a higher capital adequacy index. For the company that is procuring capital from the market by issuing stocks, R.O.A is the deciding factor. Stockholders keep a careful watch on this index. According to them, a higher R.O.A value means likelihood of a better share price of the company in future. So, it is an index that the top management usually takes a lot of interest and keeps a constant watch on it.

Improvement in the profit and loss statement is possible through the inventory management.

'The profit and loss statement' also shows the performance of the company's management. We can see how the statement changes by application of the inventory management from the Fig. 18.

Variation of P & L statement

Items	Improvement	Reasons
Sales	Can increase	Stockout disappears
S.A.E.	Can decrease	The logistic expense decreases by being able to turn with a little stock.
Operating profit	Can increase	The selling and administrative expenses decrease
Extraordinary loss	Can decrease	The stock to be disposed decreases
Net profit	Can increase	The extraordinary loss decreases

Fig. 18: Factors influencing P and L statement

We have observed that the inventory management leads to an increase in the gross profit. This is the result that the stockholders would be much interested. We find that the result comes into view through such a statement. Selling and general administration expenses include the logistic fee. Logistic fee indicates the cost of running the warehouse and the transportation. If the stock decreases, the warehouse can be small. Thus, there would be a commensurate reduction in the running cost of the warehouse. There would be a reduction in transportation also as there would be no extra stock to move.

8. There can be some direct effect expected from stock control.

The inventory management makes business operations speedy.

Let's think of the effect we can expect by having an appropriate inventory management. We can take the example of stock control of a refrigerator to have an easy understanding. The basic objective of inventory management is to control the stock. The stock, if it remains messy in the refrigerator, poses a big problem. If the stocks are set in order, no doubt, it would become quicker and easier for the household user. One can find out the necessary things without any hassles. Proper arrangement and visual identification make it even easier to use. In such a case, even a new person would be able to access anything in a very easy manner with a little guidance. For this, specifying the address of the item may come in very handy. One can spell out its location in a manner like, 'AA from the left of the shelf at the centre'. But the basic is that there must be appropriate arrangement of the goods inside the refrigerator. It may also be better to keep goods classified according to the type of things. By doing so, there can be the following benefits:

a) One can make use of the refrigerator in a skilful manner, and

b) One can also guide others to get anything in a very smart way.

This is how an appropriate control helps to have a faster operation of the refrigerator

Fig. 19: Comparison of storage of stuffs in refrigerator

Someone may think, "It is OK even if the things are not arranged in a particular order in the refrigerator". His or her feeling may be, "I know the contents inside roughly". But, quite often, we may find that such a person is spending a lot of time searching for something. This, also, may limit the use of the refrigerator to the person like him or her only. If a person arranges a refrigerator in some nice order, he or she can work in a prompt way. Even others can avoid spending time searching for things. Thus, the situation can become self-actuating type. There may not be any need to provide any detailed instruction to others for searching things. It is exactly like 'killing two birds with one stone'.

If we practice proper inventory management, we may avoid buying any unnecessary things.

We should take up an appropriate system of the inventory management. This would help us to avoid purchasing any unnecessary things. The unnecessary things may be of the following types:

a) purchasing something that is already in the stock and is not expected to run out for a while.

b) acquiring something more than its rate of demand

The example of such unnecessary buying in our daily lives is very common. "After someone buys a piece of mayonnaise, he or she may, as a matter of surprise, find a new one already available". This is a kind of an unnecessary buy. It was possible to avoid if there was a system of stock control in practice. In such a case, one may know well in advance if there is any need to buy mayonnaise or not. Such wasteful shopping often leads to the deterioration of the commodity during storage. This may even lead to its abandonment due to the expiry of the validity period. If a person does not throw away such commodities, there could be other issues. These are like a lack of taste, or health problems due to loss of freshness.

Also, we will be able to know the speed and amount of consumption when there is an appropriate inventory management. Thus, we come to know about the demand rate. Once, we come to know about the demand pattern, we can do proper shopping according to such demand. This way, we can avoid any wasteful shopping.

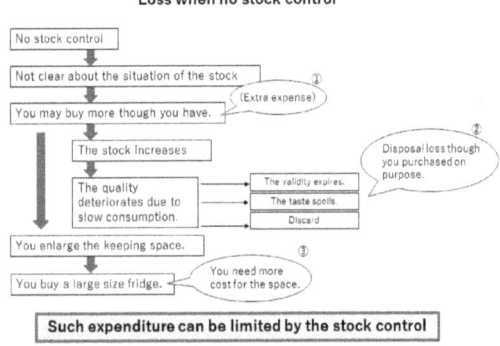

Fig. 20: How to avoid wastage due to excess stock in the refrigerator

Pocket money increases by the inventory management.

Our pocket money can increase by doing stock control. As we do not buy the unnecessary things, we can have reduced expenses. We should use up everything within the validity dates. Then, we can save on the items that might have been otherwise thrown away as wastes. In the absence of stock control, many commodities might exceed its expiry dates. This is a major cause of waste generation as explained earlier.

But often we become very concerned about 'Running out of stock'. This happens in the absence of an appropriate stock control. As a result, the amount of stock may keep on increasing. We may, then, start thinking, "Let's have a bigger refrigerator." This would result in more fixed costs as well as running expenses. More fixed costs would be there due to more investment for procuring a bigger refrigerator. There would also be an increase in the running expenses due to various factors. These factors are like increased electricity consumption, cost of maintenance etc. Thus, stock control helps in avoiding extra costs that would have occurred in the absence of it.

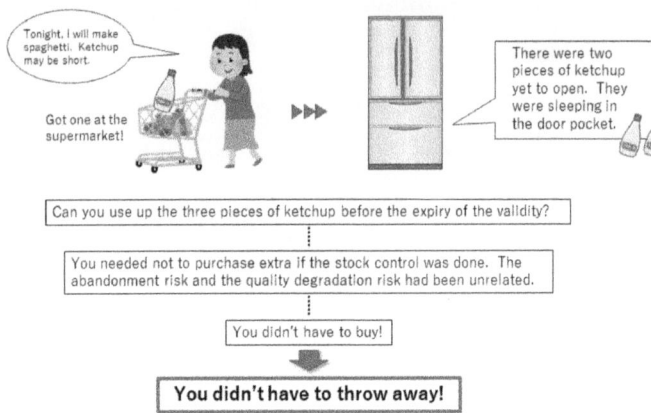

Fig 21: Negative effect of having no Stock Control

Garbage decreases when we arrange things in order during storage.

Amount of garbage decreases when we exercise stock control. To begin with, there are two things that we should take care of to get rid of any need for throwing away things as garbage:

1. Expiry of the validity date: We do not need to throw away anything as garbage if we use up all the stuff before its expiry date.

2. Some items may be safe, quality-wise. But we at times throw them away. This is due to our thinking that these don't seem to come to use any longer. It becomes wasteful if we don't use what we have.

Such abandonment may arise when there is a change in

demand due to various reasons. Demand changes occur in situations like "the change of the season" such as from summer to autumn. When environment starts becoming cold, we may not feel like taking some foodstuffs. These are like those foodstuffs that are good for summer. When we practice stock control, we may do away with such abandonment.

We are quite aware that the change of the seasons occurs in a gradual and slow manner over a period of time. We also know the things that we may not be willing to consume as another season is approaching. So, we should synchronize our stocks according to the upcoming season. If we exercise stock control, we would be able to prepare well for such changeovers. As a matter of good habit, we would keep only the necessary stock by noticing any upcoming change. For instance, when autumn is approaching, we must make a change in the stock of foodstuffs. We should replace some foodstuffs that best suit for summer season. We should take such decisions well in advance in a planned manner.

We may experience a couple of good things when we do such stock control. There won't be a need to throw away what we have bought. Also, a meaningless act of throwing away a lot of outdated things as garbage would disappear.

The work worth doing increases with the inventory control.

Now, it must be quite clear that appropriate inventory management results in a lot of good things. Also, there may be a significant impact on employees' mindset. I am going to explain this in brief in the following paragraphs:

We should think, "Will there be any family that would not be happy to undertake a system of stock control?" Any company can expect a similar effect by adopting system of inventory control. Inventory management in any organization can make company life happier and more enjoyable! There is a reason why the company life of employees would become happier. Employees have to do a lot of meaningless activities when there is a lack of inventory control. Such activities do not contribute to the sales at all. If there is a proper system of inventory management, we can avoid most of these activities. Everyone's effort, thus, would become valuable by avoiding unnecessary work. Employees, in such a situation, would be able to connect with the value addition, i.e., profit generation. Please refer to Fig. 22 and 23 below in this context!

Fig. 22: Adverse effect on operating staffs in the warehouse

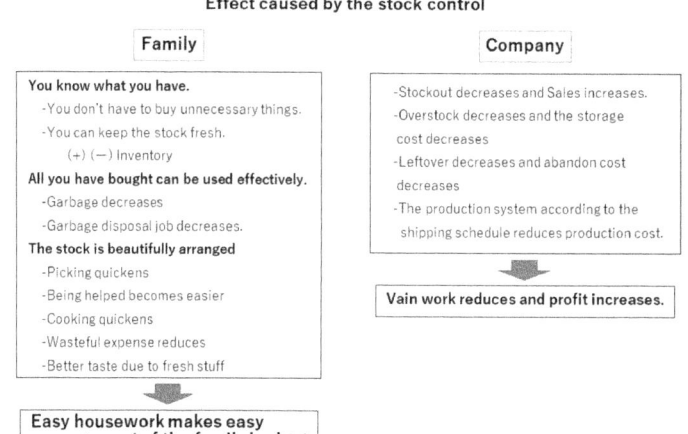

Fig 23: Results of having appropriate Stock Control

Lessons the translators have got from Chapter 1

1. Managers should pay more attention to the inventory of the company.

2. Managers should understand what would happen if there is a lack of inventory control.

3. Managers should capture data of the stock in financial terms.

Chapter 2

A company should capture its stock by the number of days.

1. How should we count the stock?

We should do stock control by the quantity, not by the amount of money.

Purpose of grasping the amount of actual stock in hand is to manage the stock. It is necessary to think about the information on 'what is necessary'. With such data, we can exercise stock control in most effective way. To begin with the stock control, the first step is to 'Set the Target'. Often, the target is set using some typical statements. An example is like: "We must restrict stock to 'XX months or days' of average monthly consumption level." Moreover, there are some companies that set a target like "The stock must be less than 'XX' yen." or "There must be a reduction in stock by 30 percent." By the way, such 'target settings' usually do not result in any concrete action. It hardly leads to the desirable results. When a management suggests the target as "Reduction of inventory by 30%", it may not sound very concrete. We can say what the management may be thinking about a rough image of the amount of money that it intends to unlock.

Often, there is a lot of variation in the prices of various commodities. Some may be high-priced commodities, and others may be much cheaper ones. Due to such variation, stock of even one piece of commodity A (of unit price, 100,000 yen) may be worth 100,000-yen. But the stock of 100 pieces of commodity B (of unit price, 100 yen) may be worth only 10,000-yen. In such a situation, it is impossible to decrease the stock of commodity A by 30 percent. So, the necessary parameter to focus on should be the "quantity of commodities lying as stock". This is instead of the "amount of money lying as the stock". Hence, it is important to gather data of quantity of stock of each commodity. Such data should have a complete break-up. For example, we should not describe a commodity like shirts of 100,000 yen. We must have the necessary break-up of this data. It should have size wise and color wise details also. Size could be S (small), M (medium), L (large), etc., and color could be white, black, etc., as shown in Fig. 24 below.

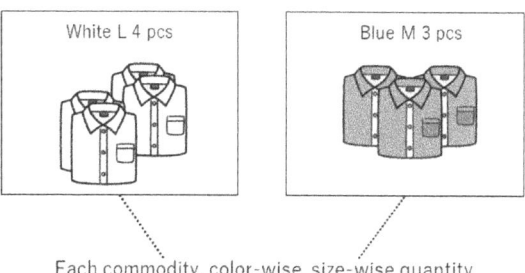

Fig.24: Break-up of each commodity is important

We should convert the quantities of stock by the number converted into days.

Let's assume that there is a stock of 5,000 pieces of a particular commodity. How do we understand whether the stock quantity is proper, or whether we should reduce it? Of course, it is not possible to judge it only from the information of the number of pieces lying in stock. We cannot say whether the stock is appropriate or not until we compare it with the sales information. The information is like how many commodities are being sold in a month or so. There are various ways to gather the sales information. It may be as "the amount of the sales in a particular year." Or, it may be as "the amount of the sales in the latest or the previous month."

We maintain stock to help in the prompt delivery of the commodities to the customer. A customer becomes satisfied when there is timely delivery of the commodity ordered. But the customer may never have any interest to learn the amount of stock the supplier may be having. "The best is to manage without maintaining any stock of the concerned commodity." We should keep this as the extreme goal in mind for stock management. But, often, it may be difficult to work with zero inventories. Let us examine the amount of the stock that we should keep in case the same is unavoidable. Most important point is that there may be a need to keep some stock for the smooth running of the business. In such a case, the general wisdom is that the amount of such stock should be as less as possible.

Following are two conditions to address the question of "the amount of the stock that may be enough":

a) "The amount of the stock necessary for prompt delivery of goods to the customer," and

b) "The most economic amount of the stock from the procurement point of view"

First, we should calculate the amount of the lowest possible desirable stock. Next, it is important to check the physical amount of the stock of the concerned commodity in hand. This is to confirm if the same is adequate for the earliest possible delivery expected. Thus, such data of sales like "how many commodities are being sold per day, of late" is also very useful. It helps in deciding the best level of the stock of various commodities. Let's now divide the stock amount by the daily sales figure. Then, we can convert the stocks in hand into "the number of days of stock in the warehouse".

Stock becomes visible if we convert it into the number of days.

The data on total shipments from all distribution centers would reveal the sales per day data. Then, we should contrast the amount of stock in hand data with the shipment data for each commodity. The best way is to use the data of sales that has a direct link to the sales to the "end customers". But it may take time to collect such data. So, we may use the shipping data of the distribution centers for the sake of prompt data collection. Let us now check the following expression:

For any given commodity, suppose,

'The amount of the stock in hand / the average shipping amount per day according to the latest sales data'

= "'XX' days" of stock.

As per the above calculation, it is possible to learn that "'XX' days" of stock are available in the warehouse. There is a rider! This is true if the shipment continues as per the current trend of sales. Suppose there are 5,000 pieces of commodity X in the warehouse and the average shipment is 1,000 pieces per day. So, what would be the answer about the number of days of stocks if we calculate using the above expression?

XX = [The stock of 5,000 pieces / the average shipment 1,000 pieces] = 5 (days of stock)

This means, there are 5-days of stock in the warehouse currently. This is judging from the prevailing shipment trend.

Suppose we only have the data of 5,000 pieces lying in the warehouse. Now, it must be quite clear that it is difficult to interpret the stock situation by this information. Suppose we convert this information into the number of days (equivalent of sales). Then, it becomes easier to be able to make the decisions. We can decide like "Let's order at once because it seems the quantity is about to become insufficient". Or "Let's leave it as it is without ordering because the available stock is enough for a while".

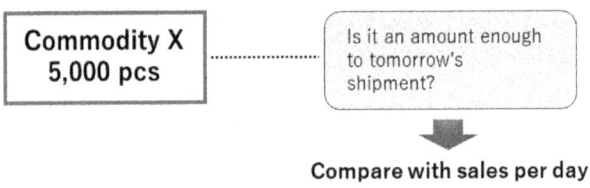

Fig. 25: To check if the stock is adequate

2. Stock quantity as the "number of days" makes the situation visible and clear.

We can understand any change of demand by "the average shipment per day".

Expressing the amount of stock in term of the "number of

days" makes it easy to interpret the stock. We can understand any change in demand pattern by "the average shipment per day". So, it is important to get hold of accurate past data of the number of shipments. The actual shipment data should be the number of shipments for each of the commodities. Each commodity means the identification up to the ultimate details of the item. It should not be the generic identification like "the stationery" or "the ballpoint pen". For instance, we should define an item like it is "the Black ballpoint pen of the BB series of the AA manufacturer". It is critical to capture such data for all the items, color-wise and size-wise etc. as may be the case.

It is because sales of any commodity might be different for different variant. For example, it is possible that "sell of a commodity of red color may not be as much as the same commodity in black color." This means that the sales vary depending on color, size, model etc. In such a case, we should not maintain the same number of the commodity as stock both for red as well as black color. So, the sale pattern is the determinant on the proper amount of the stock of each variant of any commodity.

Let us assume that the sale of a specific variant of a ballpoint pen during recent five days has been as follows:

Date	1st (Mon)	2nd (Tue)	3rd (Wed)	4th (Thu)	5th (Fri)
Shipment	6	5	6	5	7

How should we express the status of the shipment from the above data?

We must summarize the data to find out "The average shipment per day." It is 5.8 by calculation for the above case. What does this mean? It means, "There is a high possibility of shipment of 5.8 pieces of this ballpoint pen tomorrow." Let's try to understand a little more about the sale of this commodity during the next five days.

Date	6th (Sat)	7th (Sun)	8th (Mon)	9th (Tue)	10th (Wed)
Shipment	9	10	7	7	6

We observe that the rate of daily shipment is increasing a bit as compared to the previous five days. There seems to be a tendency to sell a lot during the weekend i.e., on Saturday and Sunday. The average shipment per day for these five days has become 7.8. This means that the trend of sales has now become bigger as compared to the previous week. Average shipment per day was 5.8 in the previous week. As the sales changes like this, it is necessary to capture such change of the average shipment per day. Then only we can exercise effective stock control.

Now, let us look at above mentioned sales data of all the ten days together. We should now find out the running average shipment per day during the preceding 7 days. This may be effective to assess any change of the sales during different periods of time. There may be a clear trend about any hot selling day or period. In the present example, we may find that the weekend is a hot selling period.

Date	1	2	3	4	5	6	7	8	9	10
Shipment	6	5	6	5	7	9	10	7	7	6
Ave/day		5.5	5.7	5.5	5.8	6.3	6.9	7	7.3	7.3

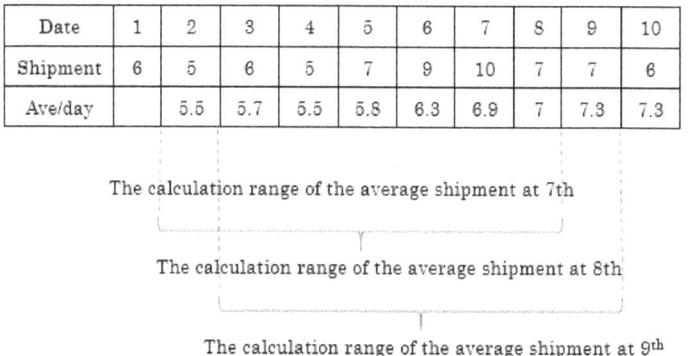

Table 3: Moving Averages of the shipment

Until the 6th (Sat.), the data of 7 days are not available. Hence, we should calculate the average shipment per day first based on all data till 7th. After the 7th, we should follow the rule of "the latest 7 days" for the average shipment figures. This is like "from 1st to 7th", "from 2nd to 8th" and "from 3rd to 9th" and so on. We call this method of calculation of running average as "Moving Average" method. This method makes us read any tendency to increase or decrease of the average. Otherwise, we may have some confusion about the daily changes. From the shipment data of Table 3, we find 7-days' moving averages as 6.9, 7.0, 7.3 and 7.3 during 7th to 10th instant. So, we can conclude that there is a marginal increasing trend of sales. But the key observation is that there is a major hike in shipment during the weekend i.e., on 6th and 7th!

We should decide the period for the study of the moving average considering:

a) life-cycle of the commodity, and

b) the characteristics of its sale.

Suppose we can have a steady sale of a commodity for a year. Then, we can choose one year for observing the range of the average. It is possible that we may expect an upsurge of demand only for a short span of time during the year. Then, we should shorten the period for study of the range of the average. It should be such that we can have an easy understanding about the change.

We can check the amount of stock by "Delivery ready days".

The shipment situation usually changes even if we maintain the necessary least stock. As a matter of fact, the demand of any commodity changes over a period of time. It's like a universal rule! Let us assume that a company is managing its sale of a certain commodity by maintaining some stock. Say, the amount of stock is 50 pieces. We should think over how to check about the sufficiency of this stock. We can do so by comparing this stock with the shipment status. Thus, the following expression holds a lot of significance:

'Amount of the stock in hand / Average shipment per day'

Let us apply this expression when the average shipment per day is 50 pieces. Then, the outcome of the expression becomes:

Amount of the stock (50 pieces) / Average shipment per day (50 pieces) = 1

This means, "It is possible to correspond to the shipment for one day by the stock available in the warehouse." This numerical value is very important for exercising stock control. We can have a very clear idea from this about the actual status. The amount of the stock and the amount of shipment may differ in most cases in reality. We call the numerical value obtained using such an expression as "Delivery ready days". Now, let us look at the situation when there is a significant decrease in the average shipment per day. Say, this becomes 5 pieces only whereas the amount of the stock still remains the same i.e., 50 pieces! Then the expression i.e., the 'Delivery ready days' becomes: Amount of the stock (50 pieces) / Average shipment per day (5 pieces) = 10

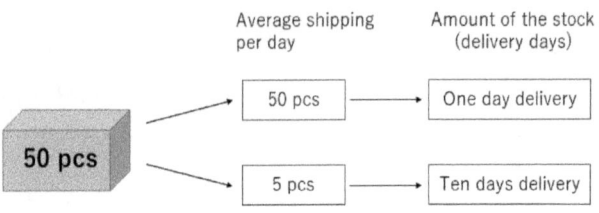

Fig. 26: Stocks in terms of Delivery Ready Days

This means, it is possible to correspond to the shipment of 10 more days with the available amount of the stock. So, we observe that the same number of stocks of 50 pieces may be adequate for "1 day-delivery" or for "10 days-delivery". It depends upon the situation of sales. So, one thing is now very clear. Managing stock quantity alone cannot help in setting a standard for stock control. Using the index of the 'Delivery ready days' helps in a realistic evaluation of the situation. We should make a regular comparison of the amount of the stock with the amount of the daily shipment.

Whether stock is proper or not becomes visible from the figure of "Delivery ready days".

One important question that may arise in our mind is, "What is the proper stock for the company?" Basic goal should be to narrow down the volume of inventories as much as possible. For this, Toyota Motor Co. adopts a system called "Kanban System".

We are sure about one thing. This is "The lesser the stock is, the better the situation is." A doubt often arises in our minds while doing so. It is, "We may not be able to respond to our customers' orders on time if the stock of the commodity is too less." There could be two contrasting situations about the sales. It could be a situation where too many commodities are going out of the warehouse. Or it could be a situation when too few commodities are only going out as sales. So, there must be an answer to the question, "To what extent can we reduce the quantity of the stock?" To find this answer, let's think about the function of the stock we expect it to perform. We have understood by now one thing that the stock is a means to respond to any order from a customer on time. It is important that we must have adequate stock for responding to any order from the customer. Only exception of this may be in the case of the "order production".

But having too much of the stock would lead to heavier burden to the management for sure. This is due to blockage of larger sum of money to arrange the stock, which, in turn, may impede the growth of the company. Following are typical implications of excess stocks:

a) A company needs cash to buy the stock.

b) It needs a place to store the stock.

c) There is also a risk of abandonment when the stock doesn't sell as expected.

This is why the lesser the stock is, the better it is. Then, there is another bigger question. It is: "Up to what level can we bring down the stock without affecting services to customers?" When there are incidences of stock-outs, we cannot think of reducing the stock. So, a company should treat stock control as an ongoing activity. This is so because the situation of sales varies over time. The company should never treat stock control like we do in a situation of a transitory disaster. When there is a hurricane or typhoon, we can say it is a state of a transitory disaster. On such an occasion, a one-time countermeasure may be enough to mitigate the situation. Of course, it may be possible to set a target in suitable terms with some logic. We can fix it in such a way that it takes care of the natural variation in customer orders. This kind of stock management can be possible by setting the target in "number of delivery-ready days". This is like "XX days of stock".

3. It is necessary to make the reality of the stock obvious.

We should capture the reality of stock of each commodity.

There is a method by which we can understand the reality of stock. This is by doing simple calculations and drawing a diagram. It is like a roentgenogram often taken during a health check-up of a person. It becomes possible to judge about health by going through one single diagram only. This diagram contains every necessary detail. We can understand at a glance from a similar diagram whether the warehouse is healthy or not.

It is not so difficult to pick up the necessary facts and figures. We must try to draw a diagram using the data of the company by all means. The best way is to determine the status of every commodity in the warehouse. But we can begin with a few vital ones. This is if taking up all the commodities in one go becomes too tough. Each commodity may have many variants. This may be color-wise, size-wise, model-wise, and so on. Then it is important to collect the data color-wise and size-wise, etc., as the case may be. We refer to the word "item" as a unique identification of the commodity.

It is necessary to collect the following data:

[First of all, we should try for one warehouse. An interesting result may come out upon careful examination of all the stocks of the company.]

1) Number of days of shipment during the month for any given item.

We need to collect the data of the shipment days during the month for all the stocked items.

1. Note down the amount of shipment of the month for the concerned items.

The expression, ② / ① = Average amount of shipment per day (say, A)

2. Amount of stock of the concerned item at the end of the month

The expression, ③ / A = Number of the 'delivery ready days'

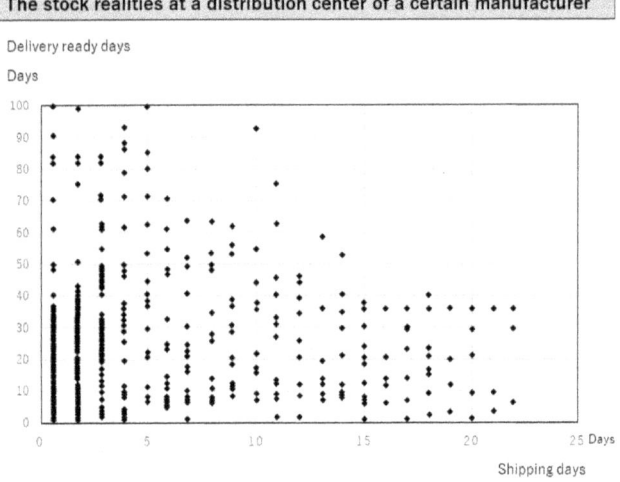

Fig. 27: Scatter plot of Delivery Ready Days vs. Shipment Days

Now, it is possible to plot a diagram (as shown in Fig. 27). In this, the vertical axis represents "the number of the delivery ready days". The horizontal axis represents the "number of the shipment days" as that of ① above. We now plot the points covering all the stocked items. It would reveal the realities of the stock of various commodities at a warehouse of a company. 'How to read the diagram' is as follows:

a) One point in the diagram shows the status of one commodity.

b) The horizontal axis shows the "number of the shipment days". The righter side of the diagram the point is, the more the frequency of shipping.

c) The vertical axis shows the "number of the delivery ready days". The upper side of the diagram any point is, the more is the amount of the quantity of the stock in the warehouse.

The problems that we can understand from this diagram are as listed below:

a) There are a lot of commodities shipping of which only occasional @ 1-2 days in the month. But these are also a part of the stocked items in the distribution centre for the customer shipment. We can also observe that the commodities shipped every day is only a few.

b) There are a lot of items that have large "Delivery ready days," but only a few "Shipping days". (Such commodities have risk of abandonment sooner or later. This may be due to lapse of its lives i.e. the expiry dates.)

c) The commodity on the top of the left in the graph

means "Delivery ready 100 days with actual shipment one day." This means that the shipping of the commodity is @ one day in the month only despite there is a stock of 100 days. In other words, there is stock to take care of delivery for next 100 months at the present rate of sales. So, the stock is for next 8 years and four months.

There was also one more problem! But this did not come to surface through this graph. There were as much as 40 percent of the entire commodities had stock. But these didn't have any shipping at all during the month.

Improvement in stock situation is possible by managing the number of the days.

We cannot learn whether there is a problem about the prevailing stock status or not from the data alone. We must check for every item with the help of the graph as explained in the preceding clause. It would be a dangerous judgment if we decide about adequacy of the stock on the basis of the delivery ready days.

Well, what can we do to improve the situation at this distribution centre? This is a distribution centre for the shipment to the customer, not a warehouse at the factory. So, the work efficiency for the shipment should be the priority. To increase work efficiency, the most important thing is not to keep any unnecessary things. First of all, there may be many commodities for which there is no shipment during the entire month. But there may be stocks of these commodities. In fact, we should notice that these don't even appear in the graph. In such a case, first, we should repatriate these to the factory warehouse. Some of these may need abandonment also due to their present state. We must not return such stocks to the factory warehouse.

We need not keep the items for a few shipment days in the distribution centre. These are items that appear on the left of the graph in Fig. 27. These items are best sent back to the factory warehouse. We should introduce a system of direct delivery from the factory when there is an order for such items. The commodities on the top left of the graph are in the situation of excessive stock and few shipment days. If we leave these items as it is, there is a big possibility of facing stagnation. So, there is a need to check every item with care without fail and take proper measures.

It seems quite logical to make some kind of rule that would not allow keeping such commodity as stock. We should fix some cut off on the number of shipping days of the month. We may decide not to keep in stock the commodities where the number of shipping days is less than 5, for instance. The graph would then look much different as compared to the one shown in Fig. 27. Refer to Fig. 28. What kind of a distribution centre would it be if we find the graph like this?

It is good to have frequent shipping and receipt of stocks in any distribution centre. We can call this a well-managed distribution centre. This is because it can keep calculated narrow amount of inventory. It is a rapid moving situation. It is fast and steady in shipping and receiving replenishment of the moving stock.

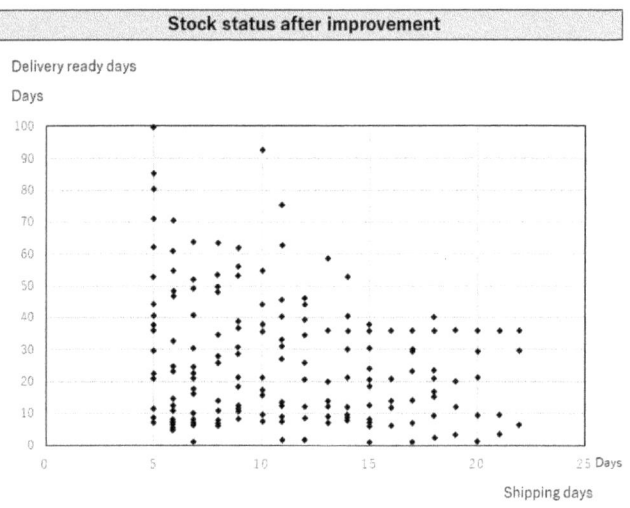

Fig. 28: Delivery Ready Days vs. Shipment Days
(After Improvement)

In inventory management, there is an important term called "Rotation". This is the time between the receiving 'in' and the shipping 'out' of the commodity. In case of the distribution centre, we must aim at "a good rotation". Such a set up ensures prompt shipment to the customer! It is not possible to altogether feel relieved by achieving a good rotation. This is even if there are a lot of shipment days. In the graph of Fig. 28, there were some commodities towards the right side. For these, the number of shipment days is high. Also, these items have a large numbers of delivery ready days. The commodities that scatter on the upper right of the graph are somewhat in a risky situation. It is because these items might become excessive if there is a fall in the shipment pace. Then, we need to set another standard for ensuring efficient stock control. For instance, it could be a standard like "We should keep at most ten days of stock in this distribution center". As a result, there would be further narrowing of the stock of the distribution center. The pattern of the graph would, then, change as shown in Fig. 29. The distribution centre can this way, become the one with a rich metabolic rate. This is due to prompt replenishment by the good rotation of all the commodities. At the same time, it ensures the least possible level of the stock.

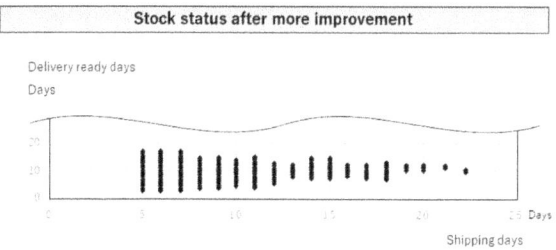

Fig. 29: Delivery Ready Days vs. Shipment Days (Best situation)

4. We can check the stock status turn-over of the inventory.

We can define the stock status by three indices.

Now, it is quite clear that the rotation can become an indicator to judge if the situation about the stock is good. Let me introduce all the three indices by which we can verify the stock status. I am going to explain their meanings as well as how to calculate these.

Turn-over of Inventory:

We define this as the number of times the commodity rotates within a certain period. Thus,

Turn-over of inventories

= Value of total sales during the chosen period/value of the average stock

It is 'larger the better'. We should calculate this index for each commodity of every warehouse.

Delivery ready months:

We define this as the number of months a commodity is 'ready for delivery' by the current stock. Thus,

Delivery ready months = 12 / Annual turn-over of inventory

It is a reciprocal index of the turn-over and hence, it is 'smaller the better'.

ROA (Return on Assets):

This is a measure of how effective is the use of the total assets of the enterprise. Thus,

ROA = [profit / total capital (total assets)] *100

Shareholders pay most attention to this index. ROA value makes it easy for them to understand about the ability of the company management. It is possible to improve ROA by the stock control as already discussed.

But these indices are not so significant at the moment for grasping of the situation. Primary aims of these are to confirm:

a) Whether the stock position is being improved, and

b) If the stock situation is at a good level or not.

It is very important there is regular checking of the stock. This is to take measures of improvement, if necessary.

Quality of the commodity also remains good if there is a good "Rotation".

A reader may not be familiar to the system of stock control. For him or her, it might be somewhat difficult to make an image of "rotation" of the stock. But it is a very important checkpoint in the world of 'stock control'. To clarify the point, let me take the example of a refrigerator. We may understand how it is preferable to rotate the foodstuffs that we keep as stocks at our homes as well.

The rotation means bringing in and moving out the content of the fridge at a particular rhythm. The key point is that any given item hardly stays in the refrigerator for more than a certain defined period. In a stricter sense, "stay" of any commodity is not preferable, though there may be a need to keep the stock. It's ideal to consume anything that is lying as stock in the fridge as fast as possible. Well, to know how many times the stock is rotating, we need to know:

a) How much quantity of stock is there in the fridge, and

b) How much of it we are using daily.

Let's examine by taking beer as a simple example. It may be too hard at this stage to calculate for all the foodstuffs lying in a refrigerator. Let's check, "Average number of bottles of beer we were having during last one month". Let us write down the same in the following table (Table No. 4) as the 'average stock level of beer'. If the figure is not known, then, let us write down the number of bottles of beer that are lying as stock right now. It was four (4) numbers on an average at my home by the way. Calculation may become troublesome due to mix up of different sizes of the bottles such as 350 ml and 500 ml and so on. In such a case, we may convert it into number of units of some standard common size to make the calculation simple.

Description	My home	Your house
Average stock level of beer	4 bottles	
Number of beers consumed in one month	40 bottles	
Turn over		

Table 4: Data of Beer bottles Availability
in the fridge vs. consumption

There is another necessary figure. It is the amount of beer consumed in last one month. Let's write this figure in the table. By the way, it was 40 bottles at my home. With these two figures, it's quite easy to calculate the number of rotations of stock.

We should divide "Number of the beer drunk in a month" by "Number of the beer stock on an average". Then, we will get to know the inventory turn-over. In my case, 'Number of Rotations (i.e., Turn-Over)' = 40 bottles / 4 bottles = 10 (turns). It means the beer turns 10 times in one month.

Description	My home	Your house
Average stock level of beer (a)	4 bottles	
Number of beers consumed in one month (b)	40 bottles	
Turn over (b/a)	10 turns	

Table 5: Data of Beer bottles Calculation
of inventory turn-over in the fridge

In general, larger this figure is the better it is. In other words, it is better when the stock turns more. What does this mean? We would understand this from the following discussion:

Let me assume that the consumption of the beer of my home increases, for instance, to 50 bottles a month. But suppose the average stock level of the beer in the refrigerator remains the same i.e., 4 bottles. Then, the stock turnover would now become as follows:

Number of Rotations (i.e., Turn Over) = 50 bottles / 4 bottles = 12.5 (turns)

This means that in this case, the bear turns 12.5 times in one month. As it was 10 turns before, it has increased by as much as 2.5 turns. What would happen when the consumption of the beer decreases? Let me assume a case when only 4 bottles are drunk during a month. And there are the same 4 bottles as stock in the refrigerator. Then, the calculation would be as follows:

Number of Rotations (i.e., Turn Over) = 4 bottles / 4 bottles = 1 (turn)

It means that the bear turns only one time in one month. The "few turns" is not preferable in the world of stock control. This is so because this indicates poor "metabolism" i.e., rate of consumption.

Note that the number of turns changes.

The change in the number of stock turns may happen even if the consumption of the beer remains same. It happens when the amount of the stock of beer changes too. Let's examine this with a simple example. Let us assume that the consumption of the beer remains the same, i.e., 40 bottles in a month. How about when there are only two bottles of beer in the refrigerator? Or how about when there are as many as eight bottles of beer due to some sudden increase?

In the first case, number of rotations = 40 bottles / 2 bottles = 20 turns

In the second case, number of rotations = 40 bottles / 8 bottles = 5 turns

It is 20 turns at stock of 2 bottles and 5 turns at 8 bottles. The rotation increases if the stock of the beer of the refrigerator decreases. This is even if consumption remains the same. The rotation decreases if the stock increases.

So, the rotation changes according to the change in:

a) Number of beer bottles consumed, and

b) The amount of the stock.

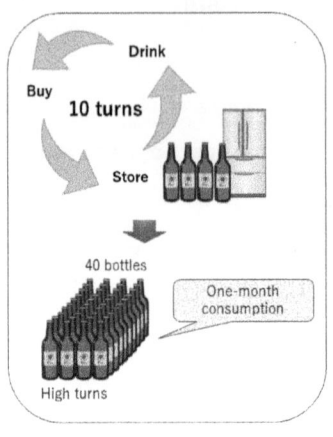 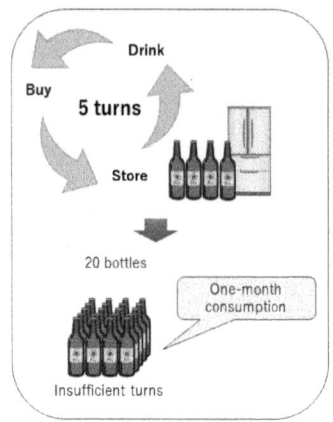

Fig. 30: Effect of change in consumption on the stock turn over

Now there are some important questions:

What would happen by such changes?

Why is higher rotation better?

When low turns	·	· Stock increases
		· Need much money at once
		· Occupy the space
		· Lose freshness
When high turns	·	· Possibility to become unsalable

Fig. 31: Study of relationship

What kinds of bad things would likely to happen with a low turn-over?

Answer to these questions may become clear from the following discussions.

Let us try to connect the related conditions listed out in the right side of Fig. 31 with the left side. In the left, there are two situations of the stocks. These are stocks with lower turn-over and those with higher turn-over. We may observe that all five conditions of the right side relate to the stocks having "the lower turns". This is as shown in Fig. 32. The situations in the right-side point towards excess stocks due to lower turns of the stock.

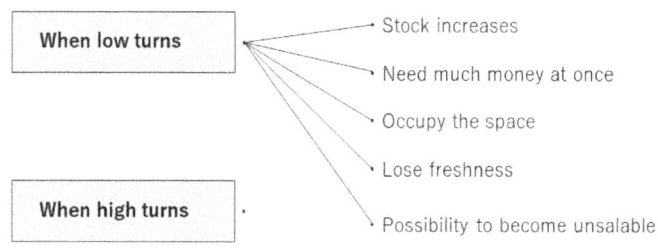

Fig. 32: Negative effects of lower inventory-turns

Let me explain in detail why it is so by using the previous example. In case, the consumption of the beer of one month is 40 bottles, and 2 bottles of beer are lying as stock. Then, it is 20 turns by calculation (40/2). In case of 8 bottles of beer in the refrigerator with the same consumption level, it is 5 turns by calculation (40/8). Well, let's see the difference between these two cases. When we calculate 30 days as one month, we drink 1.3 bottles of beer on average every day. We always maintain

2 bottles of beer as stock in the refrigerator. This means, rate of consumption is 1-2 bottles of beer every day, and replenishment of the stock is @ every day.

Hereafter, let's try to understand the following points:

    a. The norm of keeping the stock is 4 bottles at most. So, the quantity is not so big for replenishing it time to time.

    b. As we only need to but 1-2 bottles, necessary cash required at a time is also small.

    c) A small stock doesn't need big space for its storage.

    d) There can be always fresh stock.

    e) 2 bottles of stocks are enough at a time to meet the requirements. The rate of consumption is only 1-2 bottles per day with average of 1.3 bottles. At the same time, it doesn't cause any waste.

Anybody who consume beers would admit the merit of such a good rotation. It is so as it helps in having the stock of beer "always fresh." Now, there is one concern. We need to replenish the stock every day. This may cause a bit of hardship to the person who shops. Answer to this is that we must adjust it according to the cost of "Movement for shopping".

Now, let's think about the method of the replenishment of the stock @ 8 bottles of beer on an average. The beer may be available in three modes. It may be as a single piece, or with a pack of six bottles and with a case of 24 bottles. A house with an average stock of 8 bottles usually purchases a pack of 6 bottles, not @ single piece.

Suppose I buy beer at the rate of a pack of six bottles. So, when there are 8 bottles of beer in the refrigerator, the stock in the refrigerator become 14 bottles. Thus, this would occupy much more space. It will take one week or more at my home to use up the stock of 14 bottles. This is because my family consumes only 1-2 bottles every day. As about the freshness, it would be far inferior in comparison to a state of a good rotation. Besides, there is a problem that it may not remain usable always in future. For instance, it may become very cool and frozen. Then, one may not feel like drinking beer. At such time, if there are lots of bottles of old beer in the refrigerator, they may continue to remain in the fridge. In the world of stock control, it is quite dangerous. It may lead to the formation of a kind of stock that we call as "Dead stock" or "Non-moving stock".

Let's understand the core message of the Fig. 33 in the context of above discussions. Timing and quantity of the incoming stocks should match with the outgoing stocks. Any major deviation from such a balance is bound to give rise to problems. This may be either in the form of a situation of stock-outs or creation of dead stocks! Possibility of having such dangerous kind of stock is much lesser with a good rotation of the stock. Moreover, it is also quite easy to respond to some changes in the consumption pattern. Thus, taking clue from the example of refrigerator we can conclude that:

a) Buying commodities on a larger scale in any company, the stock quantity would be very high. Then, it would lead to a much bigger as well as adverse influence on the management situation of the company; and

b) Keeping situation of the warehouse in the condition of good rotation of its stock is a very welcome step. It plays a very positive role in maintaining financial health of the organization.

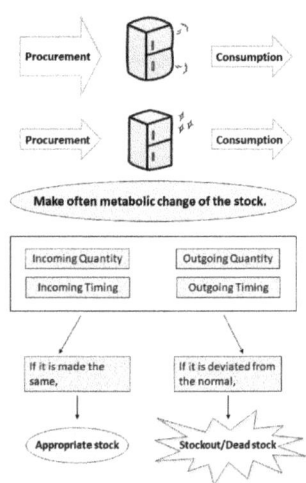

Fig. 33: Condition that leads to the situation of 'stock out' or dead stocks

5. We can understand the situation of sales by the ABC analysis.

ABC analysis of the stock helps in understanding the situation of sales.

We divide the commodities into three categories of A, B, C according to sales volume in the "ABC analysis". There are some companies that use another category, D also. This is for those commodities that are hardly sold. Some companies may consider the "Dead Stocks" as the category D commodities. In a precise sense, we can call it as the 'Non-moving dead' commodity category.

There is another way to differentiate the commodities. In this, we divide the commodities into two categories according to sales. This is very popular as the rule of "Eighty Twenty". There is a wide tendency to have a use of this rule among many companies. The meaning of this rule is that 80% of the total sales are from 20% of the commodities. Thus, these commodities rank-wise belong to the category of the higher sales.

In ABC analysis, we rank the commodities sales-wise in a descending order. The convention is to call the top 20% of the commodities that contribute to the higher sale under A category.

By use of some kind of ratio we may have a proper understanding of the sales situation.

The necessary numerical value for this analysis is the sale amount of each commodity. We then list out the commodities in the descending order of the sale amount. We further calculate the ratio of sales value of each commodity to the total amount of the sales of the company. We call this ratio so calculated as the "Composition Ratio". And then, we calculate the cumulative values. After this, we plot a graph using these cumulative values. It is common to call such a graph as a "Pareto Graph". We call the calculation table as the "Pareto Chart".

Now let me take an example of a company that handles only 10 commodities. This is to simplify the explanation. Here, I have done the ABC analysis on it. Please refer the table shown in Fig. 34. In this, I have shown the sales figures of each commodity in the left side of the table. I have arranged the commodities in a decreasing order of the amount of the sales of the commodities. The composition ratio indicates contribution of a commodity to the total sales amount. Now, let's check the column of the cumulative composition ratio in the table. Please refer right part of the table in Fig. 34 for the cumulative consumption ratios. We can observe that 79% of cumulative sales occur up to the second commodity. This means top 2 commodities contribute to 79% of sales out of a total of 10 commodities. This is exactly a case where we have achieved 80% of sales with 20% of the commodities. I have plotted a graph using the cumulative consumption ratios. A company can also make use of this plot to decide Category A, Category B and Category C of commodities by itself. By the way, this company decided to categorize the commodities as below:

a) Commodity category A until 80%,

b) Commodity category B until 90%, and

c) Commodity category C for the balance.

In the ratio of the corresponding number of commodities, we observe the following:

a) Commodity A makes up by the top 2 nos. i.e. 20% of the commodities,

b) Commodity B makes up by the following 2 nos. i.e. 20% of the commodities, and

c) Commodity C makes up the rest 6 nos. i.e. 60% of the commodities at the bottom of the table.

From this, it seems quite logical to consider dividing the entire stock into such a ratio as a standard. It is like dividing the commodities in the ratio of 20:20:60 roughly for A, B and C classification.

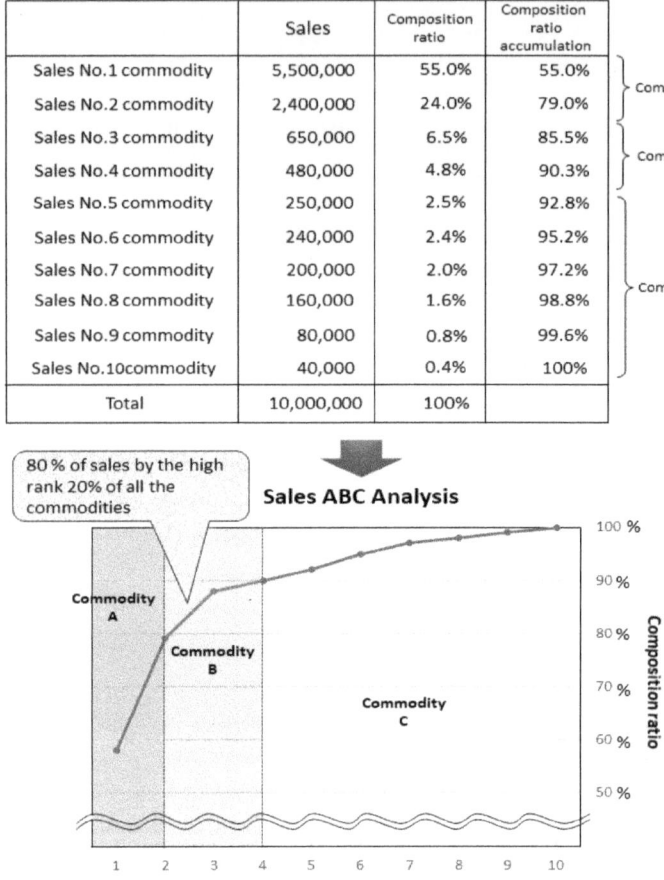

Fig. 34: ABC analysis of commodities based on sale pattern

Management methods should not be different for different commodity divisions.

There is a logic behind, 'Why do we need such an analysis? Often a company may emphasize on a close management of Commodity A. There is a strong reason. This category of commodities contributes highest to the sales. Hence, the company have a feeling that there should never be a situation of stock-out. But it is not an acceptable proposition from the business point of view.

Everyone may get convinced about the above kind of action at first glance. But there may be a pitfall in such an approach. Big emphasis on the management level of 'Commodity A' may lead to an adverse situation. There may be lower importance level in the management of other categories. These are Commodity B and Commodity C.

The sales situation of any given commodity is likely to vary over the period of time. For example, the Commodity A may move to 'Commodity B' category. Or Commodity B may move to 'Commodity A' category and so on. The management method should then differ at each different situation of the commodity composition. Thus, the process of management may become somewhat complex and troublesome. This is because there would be a constant need of checking the change of status. The changes are in the classification for the commodity category time to time. So, there has to be system to manage such changes in the control method.

In doing inventory management, we need to grasp and calculate a large amount of data. Then, only, we can exercise a strict 'stock control', But it is difficult to do all these in manual mode. It is our good fortune that the present age is an age of technological advancement. It is quite easy to deploy computer for such activity. We are now very familiar with this, and cost-wise, such deployment is also quite inexpensive.

In the present time, internet and computer services are available at ease. It is now possible to deploy suitable software on the internet, like a cloud computing. This way, the data management has now become much easier, faster as well as economic using a computer. In other words, it is quite easy to aim at exercising stricter control over the stock as much as possible. We would need to do the exercise to any number of changes in the classifications of the commodities. This is as long as a computer is managing the data and all the calculations.

I have tried to touch upon every aspect of stock control of different kind of commodities in this book. I have explained all details without making any compromise. Hope the readers like you will find it handy.

To check connection between sections by using ABC analysis of the stock

There is a key reason to introduce the technique of ABC analysis. This makes it easy to check how the connection or link is between various sections in a company. We should do ABC analysis not only for the sales but also for the stocks of the commodities.

Each commodity should have a proper amount of the stock according to its sales trend. But the connection between the sales and the stock is a vital factor to execute this concept. In most companies, the sales section and the stock preparation section are different. There must be appropriate connection between these sections. Otherwise, maintaining appropriate amount of the stock may not happen in reality.

Let us examine first the value of the stock of each commodity. Then, let's plot the cumulative composition ratio for stocks as well as sales. I have now expanded the table of Fig. 34 with data of stock of each commodity. I have plotted a graph showing the cumulative composition ratio of the stock values as shown in Fig. 35.

We can observe from this graph a particular trend. The lines of cumulative composition ratios for sales and stock are away from each other. Such a gap between the lines signifies an important thing. It reveals that there is unbalance between the Sales and the Stock. This highlights a lack of balance in procurement of the commodities. Under such a circumstance, the refrigerator may even burst due to overloading. Or, in other words, it may become unable to accommodate all the goods. This is because incoming quantities are always bigger than outgoing ones.

	Sales	Stock	Stock Composition ratio	Accumulative Composition rate
Sales No.1 commodity	5,500,000	12,800,000	42.7%	42.7%
Sales No.2 commodity	2,400,000	6,520,000	21.7%	64.4%
Sales No.3 commodity	650,000	2,850,000	9.5%	73.9%
Sales No.4 commodity	480,000	1,850,000	6.2%	80.1%
Sales No.5 commodity	250,000	960,000	3.2%	83.3%
Sales No.6 commodity	240,000	1,290,000	4.3%	87.6%
Sales No.7 commodity	200,000	860,000	2.9%	90.5%
Sales No.8 commodity	160,000	150,000	3.8%	94.3%
Sales No.9 commodity	80,000	750,000	2.5%	96.8%
Sales No.10 commodity	40,000	970,000	3.2%	100%
Total	10,000,000	30,000,000	100%	

Sales・Stock ABC Analysis

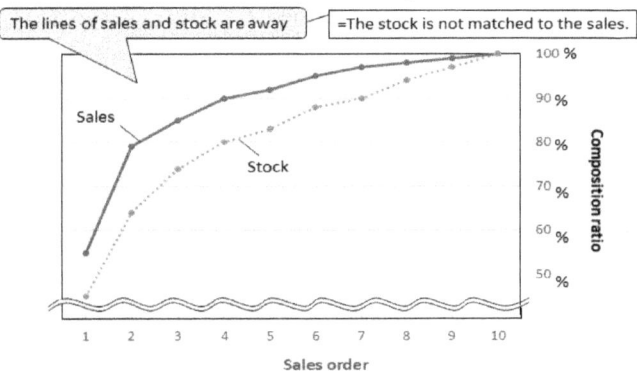

Fig. 35: Mismatching of Sales vs. Stocks ratios

6. Which stocks contribute to the profit?

To check the profit condition by the cross ratio

The "Cross Ratio" is an index. By this, we can understand how the stocked commodity helps in generating the profit. Method to calculate this is as follows:

The cross ratio = Gross profit ratio * turn-over of the commodity

The following are the basic principles in applying the above formula:

- The cross ratio is high with small stock and large gross margin.
- The cross ratio is low with large stock and small gross margin.

We may observe that a commodity with a high cross ratio can lead to earning of greater profit. But we should also understand that there might not be regular sale of such a commodity. So, it is quite clear that a business cannot flourish only with this kind of commodities.

We should divide the commodities by the profit rate and the turn-over.

It is a general practice that, in the high-priced commodity, the gross profit rate is high, and the stock is small. So, it means it is the commodity of high cross ratio. In the supermarket, the item like 'canned caviar' is one such example. But the scale of sales of this product (caviar) in the business of supermarket can only be minimal. The main constraint is that there is a limited demand. So, having plenty of the commodities of this type may not help in running the business of the supermarket.

But there is a type of commodity that is an indispensable kind of commodity in the supermarket. One such example is the fresh vegetables. For such commodity, the turn-over is usually high. But the gross profit margin (profit rate) is generally low. In fact, there are four possible kinds of the commodities. Two indices of profit rate and turn-over of the commodity can have four combinations. This is as explained below:

We can do for only a few select commodities if it's proved to be too difficult to do the exercise for all the commodities. In such a case, it is better to choose the following kinds:

   a) the commodity that seems to have the highest profit rate, and

   b) the commodity that seems to have the highest turn-over or rotation.

As a matter of fact, with such data we can set up the limits in the graph for both the vertical as well as the horizontal axis. Now, let us draw two lines:

   a) one through the middle of the horizontal line, and

   b) another, through the middle of the vertical line.

The lines are such that it divides whole set of observations into four equal sections as shown in Fig. 36.

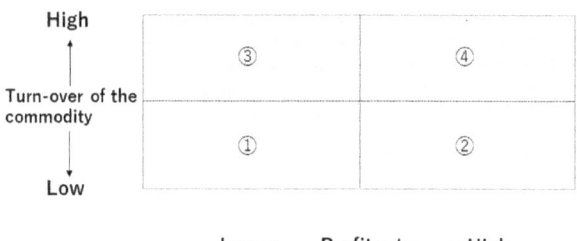

Fig. 36: Categories of commodities based on gross profit margin and turn over

We should now try to note the profit rate and the turn-over of each commodity dealt in any section of a company. Then, let's fill the data in the table of Fig. 36. For example, in case of the commodity A, if profit rate is less than average and turn-over is more than average, then, we should plot Commodity A on the area of ③. We may like to visualize a picture of the total company as well. Then, we should plot data of gross profit margin rate and turn-over of all the commodities of the company. Well, at this point, let's check how about the distribution of observations in all four sections. Four different sections of the table will now depict four types of commodities. I am going to define these as below:

Commodity significant to display:

The commodity of section ① is of low profit rate as well as of low turn-over type. Hence, the contribution to the company is the lowest. But we should consider this commodity as necessary. This is from the viewpoint of having a good assortment to complete the product basket. So, it is important to better manage these by maintaining lower level of stock as far as possible.

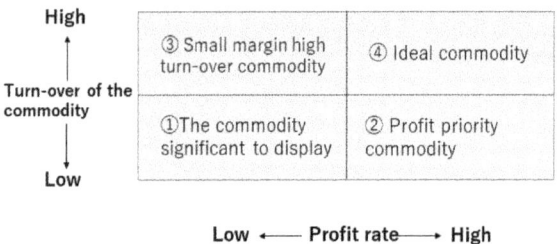

Fig. 37: 4-types of commodities

Profit priority commodity:

The commodity that belongs to section ② is of high profit rate and low turn-over type. When the turn-over becomes too much low, the contribution to the company also becomes low. Hence, it is necessary to examine if we should continue keeping stock of such commodities or not. This is especially when it falls below a certain preset standard.

Small margin high turn-over commodity:

The commodity that falls in section ③ is of low profit rate

and high turn-over type. Hence, this type is also known as "small margin high turn-over" type of commodity. There are a lot of companies that put preference on this kind. By this, companies secure higher scale of sales as well as a greater number of the customers. If the profit rate reduces by sudden rise of cost of procurement, the profit may disappear. This is so because the wage component of manpower increases with high turn-over. So, one must be very careful to ensure that the profit rate is not lower below a certain threshold level.

Ideal Commodity:

The commodity that belongs to section ④ is of high profit rate and high turn-over type. Hence, such type is an ideal or the most sought-after commodity for any management. Every management would like to wish that its most of the commodities should be of this type. But the irony is that the requirements of this type of commodity also can't always remain the same. This may be because of appearance of the rival companies dealing in the same type of commodities. Or customers may shift their preferences for such commodities. Over the period of time, there may be a situation of reaching monotony or saturation level. We call such changes in the sale pattern are due to market dynamics.

To check "A good commodity for the company"

By the way, the cross ratio is the same in both the following cases:

a) When the turn-over is 3 and the profit rate is 2%, and

b) When the turn-over is 2 and the profit rate is 3%.

The profit contribution level to the company in both the cases would also be the same. It's important that we make the best use of the commodity division based on above feature. Let's draw another line on the graph prepared earlier. For this, the first step is to fix an appropriate or preferred cross ratio and draw a line on its value. This will be a diagonal line along the left-most up to the right-most bottom as shown in the Fig. 38.

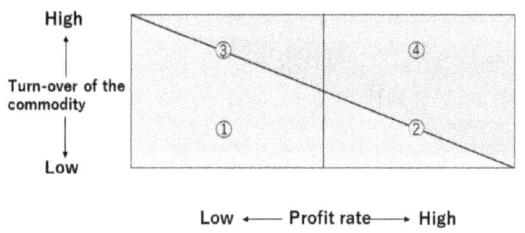

Fig. 38: Deciding about the good commodity

The commodities that appear in the upper right side of this line are preferable. These are the commodities that would contribute to a better profit range for the company. As for the commodities on the left side of the line, the profit contribution is small. Hence, such commodities are not preferable. In fact, we should try to improve the commodity on the left of the diagonal line. This way, a company can put efforts to move such commodities towards the right side as much as possible.

Lessons the translators have got from Chapter 2

1. Managers should put efforts into making the reality of the stock visible and clear. This would enable everyone concerned to understand the status at a glance.

2. Managers should know that ABC analysis is an effective means for the stock control. They should take measures according to the situation.

3. Managers should check the stock by the turn-over of the inventory of each commodity.

Chapter 3

How should we control the amount of stock?

1. "Inflow" is necessary to control by exercising stock control.

The image of the ideal amount of stock is one-day stock.

First, it is necessary to understand the situation of inventory by analyzing available data. Then, it is possible to proceed to the next important step, i.e. "How we should manage the stock". The 'ideal image' of stock is the least possible amount that is enough for the smooth running of a business. As per this analysis, we should set a target for the stock of any commodity. The best situation is, as a matter of fact, 'carrying out any business without having any inventory'. But it may look at times impractical. Hence, the ideal image may be having an amount limited to one-day stock only. The concept of stock reduction may not go well unless there is a target that looks achievable.

Let's now start with a target, "Do business with stock of one day." But there may be circumstances such that "Doing business with one day stock is impossible". Then, the best way out is to examine the situation. According to it, one may find out the least possible stock that a company can target for each commodity. We can call such a situation of inventory in a warehouse as a special or restrictive one. This is because it may not always be practical to narrow down the amount of stock to one day.

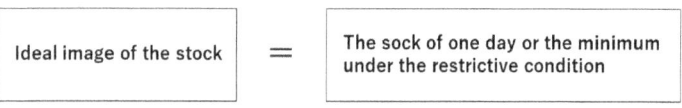

Fig. 39: Ideal Image of stock quantity

There is an implication of a restrictive condition that may be quite easy to understand. In this, there would be a need to go for a bigger amount of production and procurement. There might also be a special condition for a supplier unit for a particular kind of commodity. For example, there may be a contract that "The buying is by the case unit." This means that, say, in a typical case, even when there is a need of only 10 pieces for a day. But there may be no option but to buy at least a box or a case that contains 50 pieces. In other words, in such a case, the smallest contract unit is one case. In the case of such a commodity, we may have to have a 'five days stock' at the time of buying. This is independent of how much stock we should reduce to meet a set target. Thus, in such a case, it would be the ideal image unless business condition changes.

By the way, any company ships a commodity according to customer's order. But procurement or production is as per someone's instructions in the company. Thus, it is possible to face some issues in making shipments according to customer orders.

In a nutshell, we can say that stock control is a matter of controlling incoming goods as per the shipping data.

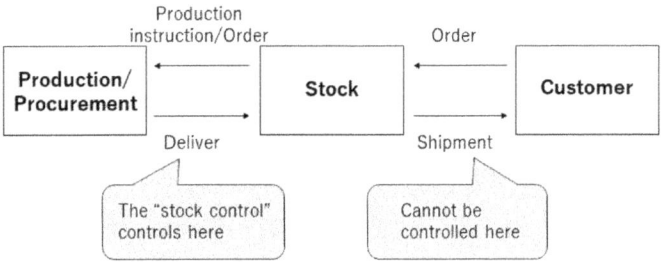

Fig. 40: Controlling of Incoming Goods is the Key!

Stock control begins with maintaining information on the realities of stock.

In what order should the process of stock control start in a concrete manner? In the case of a company, it might be difficult to see the whole image. This is because different divisions are responsible for different functions. But in our house-hold lives, we can compare 'Eating' as shipping and 'Shopping' as purchasing. Let me explain it better by taking the case of a refrigerator as an example. From this, it would be possible to have a clear image of stock control. It is easy for any organization to control the commodities it purchases. This means the 'incoming' commodities! In case of the refrigerator, such commodities are the ones "What we buy".

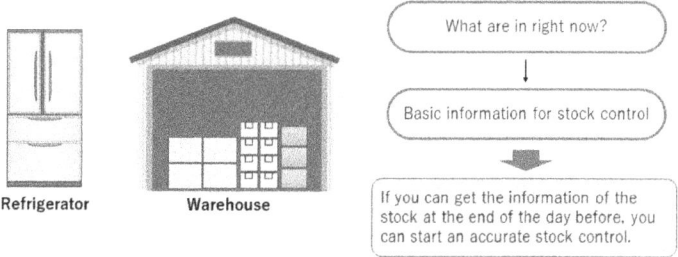

Fig. 41: Current content of the stock is most vital for stock control

So, to begin with, we need to have one most necessary information. This is, "What are the items already available there in the refrigerator at present?" In the absence of this knowledge, we cannot ensure a good shopping. From the viewpoint of "The lesser the stock is, the better it is", the good shopping is to buy only what are necessary now. We can as well say that "good shopping" means to buy only "Necessary things we may need by the next shopping time".

"What are there in the refrigerator now?" = "The current content of the stock"

This is the basic information needed for undertaking stock control. Unless this is clear, we are not ready in real sense for taking up stock control.

Checking present stock is important prior to any fresh shopping.

A refrigerator would get messy and disorganized if there were improper shopping. This is if we buy things without clear information on what is already available. We may come across the following surprises under the circumstances:

"I have bought some commodity despite I was having the same in stock;" or

"A commodity is not there in the stock. But I thought that it was available."

It is quite usual that we make a 'Shopping list' when going shopping. The purpose of this is to list out what we should buy on the particular day of shopping.

Any wise person, like a housewife, must be checking the following while going out for the procurement:

- What is already there in the refrigerator now?

- What are the necessary things already identified as outstanding to buy?

- Are there any special events expected until the next shopping?

- What are the necessary things until the next shopping considering the events?

Least required "incoming" amount is the amount until the next buy.

First step is to decide the items we need to buy. Next step is to examine the amount we need to buy. Necessary amount is "the amount necessary until the next shopping". This is considering the principle that "Stock amount should be right enough to meet the need."

Suppose we shop today and are going to do the next shopping 3 days later. Then, we have to have the things that would be necessary from today till next 3 days at the moment. We should first check the current stock of various commodities in the refrigerator. After this only we should go for shopping. If we find that:

a) There is stock of some necessary things which would not exhaust until next 3 days, we need not buy these stuffs, and

b) If we find something missing or not enough for the next 3 days, we have to replenish.

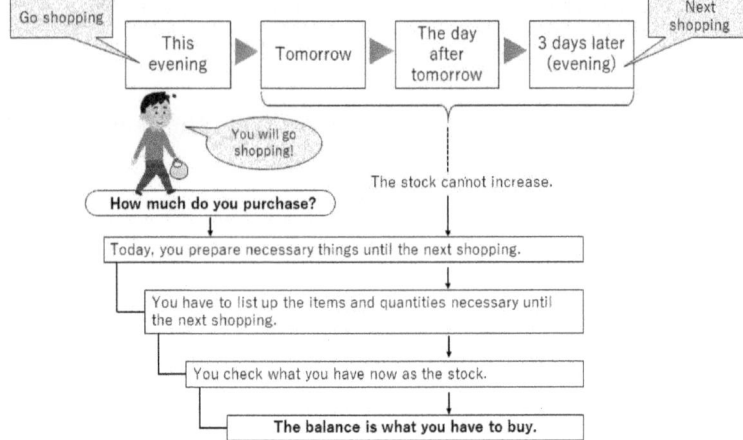

Fig. 42: Shopping cycle and calculation of things to buy

We may think that there is no need to explain such things as it's quite natural. In case, we buy the foodstuffs ourselves, we can use the logic at once without asking. In such a case, the calculation of necessary amount to buy becomes very simple. But, suppose, we get the stuffs by the mail order or by any other similar mode. Then, there is a point that we have to be a bit more careful. It takes some time from ordering to the delivery. We call this time gap as the "Lead time". Thus, it becomes an important factor to execute stock control in a successful manner. I am going to explain the lead time later in detail.

2. There are four methods of stock orders.

We must not decide the amount of the order by "KKD".

By the way, someone says that it is possible decide on the amount of order by "KKD". "KKD" is the initials of three Japanese words. It means, "Kan (Feeling)," "Keiken (Experience)" and "Dokyou (Courage)". It is a joke as a matter of fact. But it is also whispered as quite reasonable among the people who control the stock. But we can very well understand that it is very difficult to decide the correct amount of order using "KKD". We should adopt the same practice that we follow in any retail store and distribution centre. A wholesale store or a manufacturer runs such stores.

We can divide the ordering pattern into four types by the timing and the amount.

I have already described what we all can do is to control the "incoming" commodities. The critical point about controlling the incoming is: "What, when, and how many we need to buy or produce". In case of buying, we place an order to a supplier that specifies "What and how many." We call this activity as "Placing an order". A vital factor is how appropriate an order is to exercise stock control in an effective manner. Ordering method is, in general, can be of four types as shown in table 6. The basis is the two elements of ordering i.e.,

a) Order Timing (whether the ordering timing is regular or irregular), and

b) Ordering Quantity (whether the ordering amount is regular or irregular).

Methods of stock ordering

		Ordering Amount	
		Regular	Irregular
Timing of ordering	Regular	[**Regular timing and regular quantity ordering system**] To order the same quantity periodically Like one case every Monday, 1000 pcs at the end of every month	[**Regular timing and irregular quantity ordering system**] Ordering timing is fixed but the amount to order is decided examining the necessary quantity The ordering system that is being used most
	Irregular	[**Irregular timing and regular quantity ordering system**] The same amount order is placed but the timing is irregular The system in which control is made without data like "2 bin system" and "3 rack system"	[**Irregular timing and irregular quantity ordering system**] Neither order amount nor timing are fixed In some books, it has been explained as haphazard ordering

Table 6: Four types of ordering

3. Type 1 Ordering method for stock control (1)- regular timing and regular quantity

"EOQ" is an order method followed by only a few companies.

The oldest scientific technique is the 'regular timing and regular quantity' method. It is a method that takes care of "Economic Ordering Quantity (EOQ)". This technique is a major one that everyone has got some basic idea. This is true for the person who has studied the subject of stock control.

But ordering with "Regular timing and regular quantity" is not so general now. It seems that the company and the situation where there is use of EOQ method are few. EOQ is a technique that focuses on:

"How much amount and how much time interval would lead to the least ordering cost to the company".

It is to order a fixed amount at some fixed predefined time interval. This is like ordering some commodity every Monday or at any other fixed time interval. There was a publication of a literature on inventory control by W. Evert Welch in 1960. The name of it is "Tested scientific inventory control". After this, EOQ has become popular as a scientific stock control method in many companies. This has, in fact, worked as a starting step in some companies around the world including those in Japan. It was being used in business houses in the United States in 1920's as a formula of stock control.

Use of EOQ is for the commodity of which sales amount during the year is clear.

We adopt EOQ method when demand of commodities under consideration is steady. Also, when volume of its sales during the year is definite or predictive. In the good old time, there used to be selling out of all commodities produced. Thus, there might have the practice of procuring the inputs by resorting to EOQ method. Nowadays, the situation may be quite different. It is possible that there are some commodities that are never looked at. This is even though there may be display of these in the store. In such a situation, ordering with "Regular timing and regular quantity" would not work. In fact, sales trend is irregular and unpredictable in most cases in the present age. This is due to the complexity and cut-throat competition in the marketplace! Thus, we can conclude that EOQ method is very famous as a well-known stock control technique in the world. Yet, it is applicable in only a very few situations at the present time.

EOQ aims at keeping total cost of ordering to least.

From any prior experience of using EOQ, one can infer that

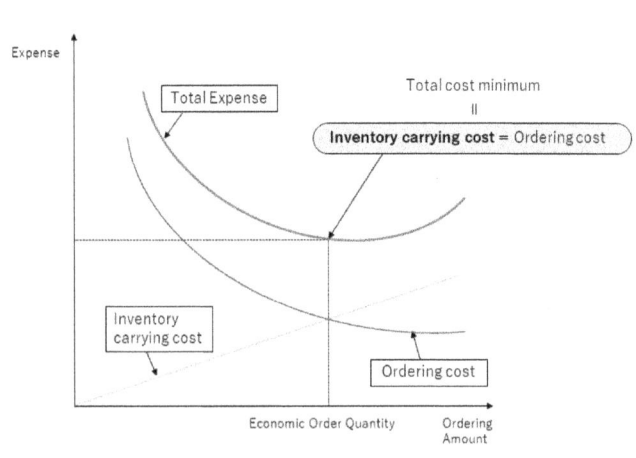

Fig. 43: Concept of EOQ

EOQ is the technique that focuses on the least possible total cost in management of stock. In EOQ, we calculate the total cost as the sum of a) ordering cost and b) inventory carrying cost. These two costs have a nature that one decreases if the other increases. Please refer Fig. 43. Its vertical axis denotes the 'cost' and the horizontal axis denotes the 'amount per order'. There are separate curves for ordering cost and inventory carrying cost in the graph. The total of these costs is also shown in the graph as 'total expense'. It is easy to understand that the least total cost comes at a point in the graph. This is the point where the ordering cost and the inventory carrying cost are having the same value. We call the corresponding amount of order at this point as "Economic Order Quantity (EOQ)."

Let's compare the ordering cost with the inventory carrying cost.

Well, let's see contents of cost calculations in EOQ in detail.

1) Ordering cost

The ordering cost includes communication expense, labour cost, and goods receiving cost. It is hard to think it as too high a cost. In case of electronic transactions with customers, the cost per order becomes insignificant.

2) Inventory carrying cost

This is the interest component over the stock a company

carries. It is the amount of money lost by way of the interest on the amount of money used to build the stock. It may also include the risk of the product obsolescence due to the stock's becoming old. There may be a fall in the price of the commodities stocked as well. There is another school of thought that we should also include the storage cost. But it is not practical to change the area of the warehouse according to the change in the stock of one commodity. This is why there is no meaning in considering it as a factor of 'inventory carrying cost'. It hardly depends on how we order the commodities. The only cost that changes depending on the frequency of the order is the interest over the stock. Thus, this is the only cost we should compare with the ordering cost.

When we are examining like this to work out EOQ, doesn't it appear somewhat unnatural? In this case, we are comparing two different things i.e., interest amount lost due to stock vs. ordering cost. It seems that we can have least inventory carrying cost by minimizing the stock interest. This is unless the ordering cost is a substantial amount. We may use EOQ method to decide the amount of production and procurement on the basis of the demand. This is under certain condition. The condition is if the demand is very much steady. Thus, we can apply EOQ method if we have a useful logic like this considering various aspects!

4. Type 2 ordering method for stock control (2)- irregular timing and regular Quantity

"Two-bin system" enables visual management.

Method of "Regular timing and regular quantity" ordering is not likely to be useful at present. But "Irregular timing and regular quantity ordering" method is still in use. There is a method called "Two bin system." In this method, we prepare two containers of the same amount of any given commodity first. Then, we put to use one container. It becomes empty upon using up all the commodity it contains. Then, we place an order for another container. In this method, we place an order only when we use up stock of one container. So, it is about placing an order in irregular timing. In this, we order a container of the same amount every time whenever there is a need. So, it is a type of 'regular quantity' ordering.

It is an excellent technique to regulate the stock using visual control. There are a lot of cases in which this method is being followed. This is so because there is no need to collect data for stock control. The method is very simple and any incidence of stock-out hardly occurs. It is a very effective method especially when it is difficult to capture the data such as:

a) 'What is the amount of stock now,' or

b) 'What is the average shipping per day'.

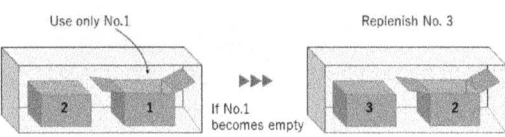

Fig. 44: Operation of 2-Bin system

Over stock / stock out is hard to be found in the two-bin system.

There are some limitations in the two-bin system. There is a possibility that:

a) Nobody notices even though operation may be going on with excessive stock, or

b) The situation may be very close to face occurrence of stock-out because no one is looking at data.

In this, the volume of stock is bound by the accommodation of container. This is the basic cause behind above kind of problems. For instance, let's assume that the accommodation of container used is 100 pcs. There may not be any problem when shipping is going well. Suppose there is shipping of only one piece during a week because of a sudden fall in demand. Still, we would need another 100 pcs if one container becomes empty. Stock of these 100 pieces in this case becomes excessive. This amount of stock would be enough for as much as the next two years of shipping. The conventional wisdom is to decrease the ordering amount if the demand decreases. But this method is a method that doesn't impress upon such a way of thinking. As a result, sometimes, this causes operational troubles. So, we should know that there is a danger of using the two-bin system in certain situations. Another example is when we need to handle a large amount of a commodity with a high unit price. But it is an effective method in the following conditions:

a. We can use it at warehouses and distribution centers where data is hardly taken.

b. We can use it for the commodity with less shipping where we may like to pay least attention.

c. We can use it for cheaper commodities. This is when there is hardly any problem in management of the company even if there is excessive stock.

The above discussion focuses on stock control of the final products. But we can also have effective use of this method in the areas like supply of parts to the assembly in factories. In Toyota, we can find use of this method. They supply parts by this method and replenish it @ once every 15-30 minutes in the assembly lines. (Translators' addition)

But it is also important to check on regular basis whether the capacity of the container is proper or not. We can do so by comparing with shipping performance. A company often put in constant effort in trying to cut short the accommodation. To this effect, companies undertake the Kaizen drive as normal practice. Furthermore, we may need to have some kind of visual check. It is to address situations like "Are there any stock stagnating in the warehouse?" or "Is the stock getting dirty due to exposure to dust and dirt?" In Toyota Production System, there is a saying, "Cleaning is Inspection." It is important to make a habit of cleaning by putting internal efforts. We never should leave it to out-sourcing.

The "3 Rack System" can do away with the uneasiness of stock-out.

In the two-bin system, we have to correspond by one container during the time between order and supply. But, in such replenishment process, there could be some waiting. A longer waiting time may cause stock-out of the commodity. To overcome this limitation, there is another method called the "3 Rack System". In this method, the system is to provide three racks. There is same amount of stock in each rack.

The operative principle remains the same as that of the 'two-bin system'. There is an order of one rack when one rack becomes empty out of three. The key difference is that in the "3 rack system" there is one more rack. This is an extra stock to get rid of fear of any possibility of stock-out. It may happen due to more time gap in replenishing the empty rack. Thus, this "3 Rack System" helps in decrease in the uneasiness due to any incidence of the stock-out. But, in this method, possibility of generation of excessive stock might arise.

5. Type 3 ordering method for stock control (3)- irregular timing and irregular quantity

"Irregular quantity ordering" becomes the basic of the stock control from now on.

We need stock control to meet change in the demand rate. The basic thinking is that it is preferable to be more flexible to the change of demand. We should have "Irregular quantity ordering" in such a way that there is only order of a necessary amount. Such amount is corresponding to the change in the demand. But it is important to capture accurate data and calculate the quantity in a prompt manner. This is to keep an eye on the change in the demand and then, prepare an order corresponding to it. There is a critical condition to adopt the "Irregular quantity ordering" method. There has to be an environment to be able to capture the shipment data of every day to the next day. For this, it is important to track stock data by use of a computer and information technology (IT). Let's check Fig. 45 to make an impression about the kind of environment we need!

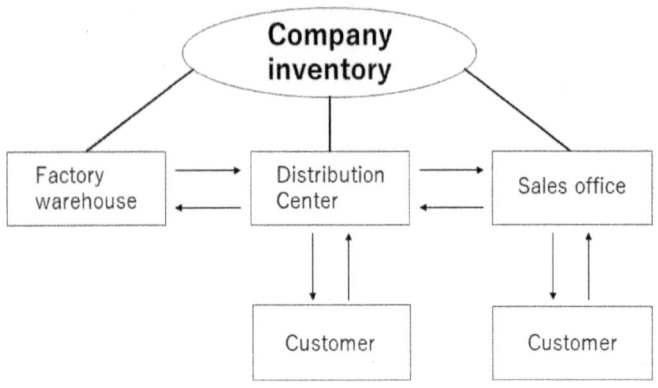

The environment where daily movement of the stock can be captured is needed.

Fig. 45: Typical environment for stock control

There is most flexibility to change in "irregular timing and irregular quantity" ordering.

Best method in the present time is "Irregular timing and irregular quantity ordering". In this, there is flexibility of change in the quantity as well as in its timing according to the demand. But there have been a lot of misconceptions about this method even now. There are some remarks about this method like, "It is nonsense!" or "We can never consider it as an ordering system!" it is a carefree ordering method without any standard. But, as a matter of fact, it is a big misunderstanding.

The basic aim of stock control is to correspond to the change of demand. So, flexibility to any change of demand is very important. This system of ordering involves watching of the change in more careful manner. It is more accurate than other methods. This is so because, there is placing of the order at the time and quantity needed.

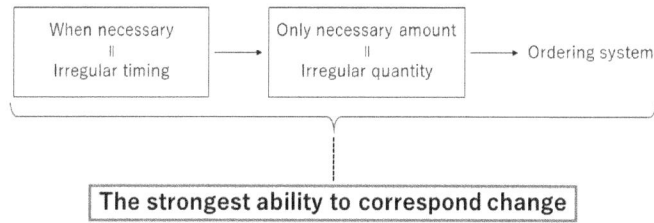

Fig. 46: Advantage of "irregular timing and irregular quantity ordering"

Computer and IT has made "irregular timing and irregular quantity ordering" possible.

Accurate information of shipping amount and stock amount in hand are most important. Otherwise, the method of "irregular timing and irregular quantity ordering" cannot hold water. The method of "Irregular timing and irregular quantity ordering" was of no help in the past. This is because there was no support available at that time in the form of a computer. Thus, it was not as easy as today. This is why people used to ignore this kind of ordering method.

In this method, it is necessary to capture the information of shipment and stock on the real time basis. Otherwise, it is not possible to calculate either the necessary amount or the timing. These are two most important bits of information necessary to practice this system. But it is quite easy to have such data available in the present age. First, computer system is widespread. In the stock data, it is quite easy to input any change very fast. It is also easy to collect stock data in the distribution centre using a computer terminal. Next, it is very easy to share such information. Stock control becomes most effective when it is undertaken for the entire company. There may be stock bases of a company across the whole country or all over the world. Even then, it is possible to capture the current stock information. This becomes possible through the access to a suitable computer terminal. It may appear that such a network is available only for the big enterprises. But even smaller enterprises can construct necessary information network by use of internet. Thus, it becomes possible to share the information across the entire company as well.

IT revolution has proved to be very revolutionary in the world of 'stock control'. This has happened sometimes around the year 2000. Now, there is a technology called "Cloud Computing". It has made more advancement in the computerization. The whole system is far more economic and faster. This has made the environmental preparations of stock control easier too.

6. Type 4 Ordering method for stock control (4)- regular timing and irregular quantity

We can use this method if there is a restriction in the ordering timing!

Many companies use "Regular timing and irregular quantity ordering" system as a method. Manufacturing companies select this ordering method to determine the production volume. In this, there is a fixed timing of ordering. Wholesalers and retailers also may use this method. This helps in making their business schedule easy due to the fixed timing of ordering. In this method of ordering, there is a fixed timing of ordering. But the amount of ordering can vary according to the situation. For instance, there may be a company who makes production schedule on monthly basis. They prefer to place the production order once a month. They do so by deciding on production items and its amount for the next month by the 15th of the current month. In such a case, there is a limitation. They can place no order for the next month's production in advance. This is so because the ordering timing had already passed. But there may be knowledge of a possibility of more sales of something in the second half of the present month. They cannot consider any such sudden need of sales for the corresponding production. Thus, there would be no alternative but to postpone the production for the month to the subsequent month.

There is no such problem in the 'Irregular timing and irregular quantity ordering'. This is because the ordering timing is not fixed. It is very difficult to determine need of the exact amount of the order by calculation on the basis of sale trend. This is where there is a restriction in the 'regular or fixed timing' ordering system.

Amount to order in the "Regular timing and irregular quantity ordering" needs prediction.

Calculation of the amount to order in this kind of ordering system is difficult. This is because ordering is @ fixed timing basis, such as once a month or once a week. In this, there is a need to think about the sales trend of near future. Thus, it involves the process of prediction.

When we determine the amount to order by calculation, it is common to use actual data. In such way, we can decide on the order quantity with a clear logic. But when we use prediction process, various kinds of errors are bound to come in. Such errors are like buyer's speculation, expectation, experience and intuition. Pressure from the sales department etc. are also other sources of errors. Following are the steps to determine the amount to order in this kind of ordering system:

First step is to predict the amount of shipping. This is until the time when we order the goods. Past shipment trend, in this case, becomes the basis. Ordering quantity is then obtained by subtracting the current stock from it. As there is a need to predict, one may feel somewhat insecure or nervous. This is even if there might be a detailed analysis of the past data. The person may feel like, "The amount (i.e., quantity so predicted) may be insufficient." So, there is a natural tendency to order much more than the quantity needed. This is to get rid of any uneasiness that may be there in future due to any stock-out. As a result, there lies a constant fear in the mind of the concerned dealing officer. There is every possibility to have excess stock.

7. Let's reduce stock by switching the ordering method.

"Irregular quantity" to "Proper quantity" and "Irregular timing" to "Proper timing"

We may find that all four ordering methods are in practice by different companies. But relative merit does not seem so easy to read by use of the terms 'regular' and 'irregular'. Let me introduce another concept replacing these terms in this book from now on. I use "Proper quantity" in place of "Irregular quantity". Likewise, "Proper timing" in place of "Irregular timing" as shown in Fig. 47. By this concept the negative image associated with the term "irregular" disappears. Hence, it makes it easy for the good points of each ordering method to come to the surface.

		Ordering quantity	
		Fixed	Not fixed
Ordering timing	Fixed	Regular timing and regular quantity ordering system	Regular timing and irregular quantity ordering system ↓ Regular timing and proper quantity ordering system
	Not fixed	Irregular timing and regular quantity ordering system ↓ Proper timing and regular quantity ordering system	Irregular timing and irregular quantity ordering system ↓ Proper timing and proper quantity ordering system

Fig. 47: A new concept that replaces the term "Irregular"

Let's examine how to switch to "Proper timing and proper quantity ordering system".

There are companies that re using "Regular timing and proper quantity ordering system". Most of them should be able to switch to "Proper timing and proper quantity ordering system." For instance, suppose a company has adopted a system of placing the order every Monday. It might have done so because the ordering work might need a lot of paperwork. It is very difficult to understand the current shipping status of each item. It is also not easy to examine information about each item from one week to one month ahead. Thus, accurate calculation of the amount to order becomes difficult. This is due to the process of the prediction involved. Furthermore, there is a need to capture the current stock. So, by fixing like "the AA day is the ordering day," company prepares its staffs to place orders. Let us now look at the situation in a different way. Suppose a company is having necessary IT support. Then, it becomes easy for the company to have a suitable inventory control system. Using the computer system, the company can calculate the above-mentioned information at ease. It is also possible in such a scenario that the company can calculate the data every day. In other words, there is no need to spare time for ordering work. So, the company should be able to switch to the "Proper timing and proper quantity ordering system". It has nothing to worry about the business or workload. In fact, it would even be possible to place order every day, if necessary.

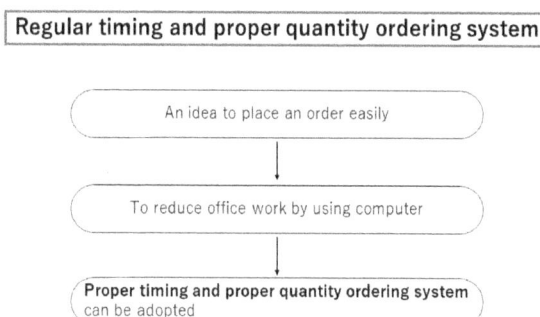

Fig. 48: Idea behind "Proper Timing Proper Quantity Ordering" system

Suppose a manufacturer has a system to make production plans monthly or weekly basis. For such a company, it is difficult to switch. But it is important to switch over to the

"Regular timing and proper quantity ordering system". So, the company may do so in a gradual manner over a period of time. Also, there is another big advantage by having this system of ordering. By shortening the period of production plan, there would be a large reduction in the amount of stock. For example, the company may go from monthly plan to weekly plan, and from weekly plan to daily plan.

8. Decision about the timing when to order is on the basis of calculation.

Lead time of delivery becomes an important point.

How do we have to calculate timing for ordering in case of 'irregular timing' ordering system? In this method, the ordering timing is not fixed. Let's think about mail or web ordering at home. Let us assume that we are obtaining rice by direct delivery from a farmer. The farmer delivers it by a week from receipt of the order. We call this period from the ordering time to the receipt of goods as "Lead time". Lead time is a promise of buyer. The supplier decides about the time duration required to make goods available. A buyer has to place an order at an appropriate time, recognizing this period. Thus, ordering timing changes according to the length of lead time. Let us refer Fig. 49 to learn how lead time changes in different circumstances!

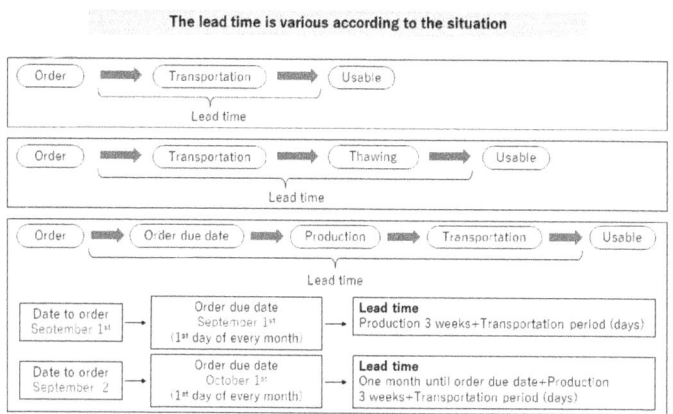

Fig. 49: Factors that influence Lead Time

It may be the case that the lead time has some range like "3 days to one week". So, we should place an order considering the worst case. Suppose we place an order at the time when there is stock of rice of 4 days only. This may be on the basis of our favourable past experience that there would be delivery in 4 days. Then, if by chance, we receive the goods are by the lead time of one-week, there would have no rice for 3 days.

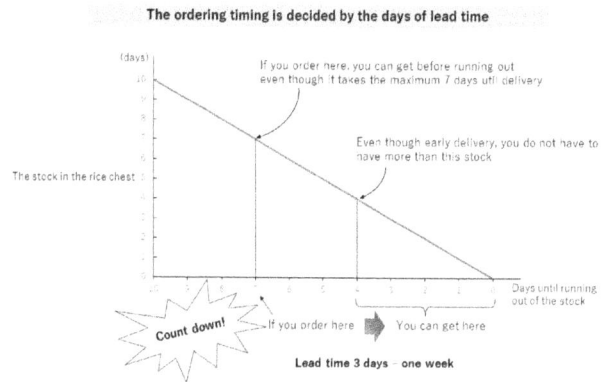

Fig. 50: Lead Time vs. Ordering Time

If we forget about the "Back Order," excessive stock or dead stock might happen.

When there is a time lag between the release of an order and the receipt of goods, we have to be careful. We must not forget that we already have an order pending for delivery. If we forget this, there would be generation of excessive stock at such instance. How about the situation if we buy some rice from a supermarket? Consider that we have also ordered for direct delivery of rice from a farmer! It may so happen that we are yet to use up the rice bought from the supermarket. But, meanwhile, we receive another consignment of rice from the farmer. In such a case, we need to be careful about the space required to store this extra quantity. Over and above, there may be deterioration in the quality of rice due to longer storage duration. In the world of stock control, there is a term called as "Released order" or "Back order". This is when we place an order, but the goods are not received yet against this order. We call such order as the "Back order." At the time of calculating 'what quantity to order', it is important to include the "Back order".

There is a key to decide whether we should place an order on a particular day.

Suppose a company is using "Proper timing and proper quantity ordering system." Let's see its order situation. Business schedule of this company is as follows.

a. The person-in-charge of ordering is to do this job as the first thing in the morning.

b. During this time, the amount of stock he confirms is the one at the end of the previous day.

c. The shipment of the day is not possible to determine at this point of time. This is because the system may still need to add: a) Accepted orders of the previous afternoon, and b) Accepted orders of the morning of the day under consideration.

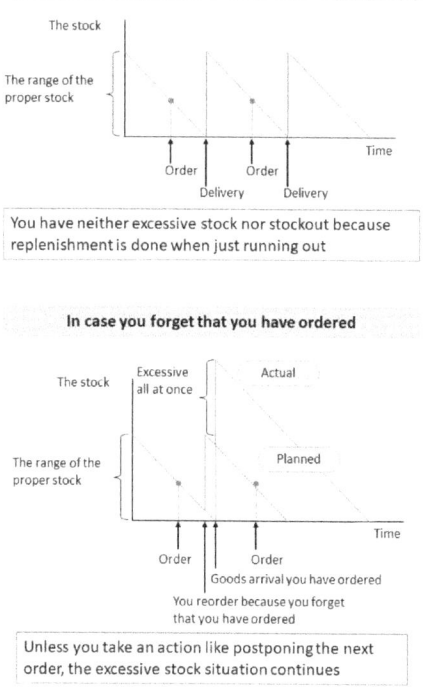

Fig. 51: Importance of keeping in mind about the "Back order"

To calculate whether to order, the first requirement is to capture the delivery ready days. One has to have this by converting the amount of stock in hand into days by use of the following expression:

Color-wise / size-wise amount of stock in hand / average shipment per day = 'AA' 'delivery ready days'

For instance, let us assume that there are 30 pieces as stock of "Ballpoint pen red 0.5mm." Suppose the average shipment per day of it is 30. Then, "the delivery ready days" is only one (1) day by the following expression:

Delivery Ready Days

= Current stock 30 pieces / Average shipment per day 30 pieces

= 1 (One) delivery ready day.

We also term it as 1-day stock. Considering the current shipment trend, the stock may run out today itself. As a matter of fact, it is very important to place an order in a hurry in such a scenario. Under such a situation, one may have to raise a special request to the supplier. The request may be to deliver the commodity immediately. But the supplier may respond by saying that it would be available only by the next day evening. With this, the accepted orders of today and tomorrow might face the problem of execution. There is a clear possibility of the situation of stock-outs. So, considering only the "Delivery ready days" cannot make the best ordering.

Decision about the date or time of ordering is going by the 'lead time' period.

Lead time is important to decide on the appropriate time of ordering. It should be in a way to avoid any situation of stock-out. When the lead time is "2 days" and we order when there is zero stock, we will have a stock-out for two days. So, it is necessary to order two days before the stock gets exhausted (i.e., before 'out of stock' situation). As we know, the average shipment per day, double of this is the amount of the "two days stock." When the amount of the stock touches the level of the "two days stock", it means that the time has come to place an order. We call this time when we should order as the "Ordering point". We can calculate it using the following formula:

Ordering point = Lead time (days) / Average shipment per day

We should note some finer points about the lead time. Isn't it that "The lead time is vague"? Stock-out happens if goods don't arrive as scheduled. There is placing of order based on the lead time. It is necessary to promise customers with clear background knowledge about such uncertainty. Moreover, it is necessary to note about "long lead time" of some goods. There may be sudden increase in demand during the period of the long lead time. As a result, there may be reduction of stock from its desired level. To bear with such a situation, there is a need to consider shortening the lead time. In another situation, there may be decrease of the demand. So, there may be increase of the stock from its desired level.

It is preferable to decide the ordering amount by the replenishment frequency.

At the ordering point, let's assume that we place an order for "AA days' amount". This indicates the number of days for the stock.

Ordering amount = days for the stock * average shipment per day

A company decides on the "Days for the stock" as per its conditions of business and intent. Its least value is "one day of the stock." If there is a decision to have "the days of the stock" as "one day", stock amount can be at the minimal level. This means that there is a need to release orders almost every day. Thus, there will be a replenishment of goods also @ every day. Likewise, suppose we decide the "days for the stock" as "one week". Then, we need to do ordering generally @ once a week. Whatever the number of days of stock decided, the ordering point moves when the rate of demand changes. Thus, the timing of the ordering becomes difficult to keep fixed as per the schedule. We calculate the ordering amount by the above-mentioned expression. This is as per the order of the sought days decided.

Let's calculate the amount of order.

The secret to have success in exercising stock control is to place an order in a correct manner. This is in respect of its timing and quantity. I have prepared an exercise for it as shown in Fig. 52. Please check using a calculator. We need to find out the numbers at ①, ②, ③, and ④. Let's try to confirm that the stock control exercise is a repeat of a simple mechanism. It is about:

a) Understanding of the current shipment status,

b) Judging whether the ordering point has come, and

c) Placing an order for the necessary amount.

The lead time is various according to the situation

	1	2	3	4	5	6	7	8	9	10
Replenishment (Pcs)					45			④		
Shipping (Pcs)	19	14	15	15	14	16	17	18	12	13
Stock Balance (Pcs)	48	34	19	4	35	19	2	29	17	4
Average shipment per day(Pcs)	14	15	16	16	15	15	15	16	15	15
Delivery ready days (days)	3.4	2.3	1.2	0.3	①	1.3	0.1	1.8	1.1	0.3
Released order (days)			2.8	2.8		3.0	3.0		3.2	3.2
Ordering point check (days)	3.4	2.3	4.0	3.1	②	4.3	3.1	1.8	4.3	3.5
Ordering amount		45			③			48		

Fig. 52: An exercise on ordering quantity, replenishment quantity, etc.

[Rules of calculation]

- Average amount of shipment per day:

  Consider it as the moving average of the latest 5 days shipment

- Amount of the stock: 3 days

- The rule to order: To order 3 days-stock when the "delivery ready days" comes less than 3 days

The answers and how to solve are as follows:

Ans. of ① is 2.3 [balance of the stock 35 / average shipment per day 15]

Ans. of ② is 2.3 [① + Back order 0]

Ans. of ③ is 45 [To place order when the ordering point comes down under 3. Quantity = the average shipment per day 15 * the amount of the stock 3]

Ans. of ④ is 48 [as the lead time has passed after the ordering, ordering amount = replenishment amount]

The mechanism of "Proper timing and proper quantity ordering system"

Let's see the movement of a goods if ordering is by "proper timing and proper quantity ordering system". Information related to the stock of this goods is as follows:

- Lead time: 2 days

- Amount of the stock: 3 days

To begin with the exercise of stock control, we should start with finding out the sum of:

a) 'Amount of the stock (3 days)', and

b) 'Lead time (2 days)'. stocks

In the graph shown in Fig. 53, the left end is the starting point. We have understood that we have 5 days stock in this case. The straight line shows the amount of stock in "delivery ready days". What we have to check always is the status of this "delivery ready days." Let's understand the movement of the stock shown in the graph. Then, we can understand the "proper timing and proper quantity ordering system". Let me explain how to read the graph in a little more detail.

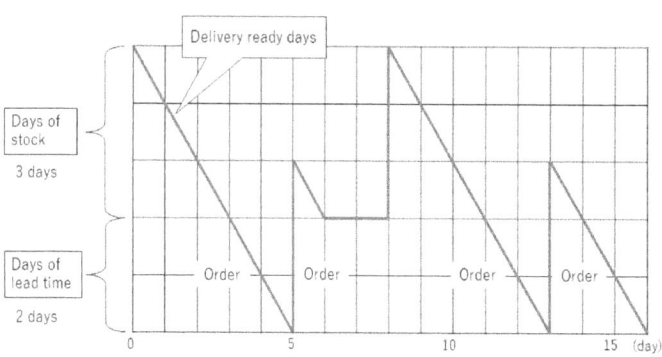

Fig. 53: Movement of the stock in proper timing and proper quantity ordering system

First of all, the smallest cell represents "one day" in both the vertical and horizontal axes. At the first day (day 0), there are 5 days stock. But on the third day, the "delivery ready days" becomes 2 days because the shipping has continued. As the lead time is "2 days", we place an order when the "delivery ready days" get reduced to "2 days". Amount of ordering is the amount of stock for 3 days. When shipping continued on 3rd day and 4th day, "the delivery ready days" came down to zero. But we have ordered the '3 days stock' two days back. We are going to receive this replenishment stock on the 5th day. So, there will be 3 days' stock available. Shipping is continuing and as a result, on next day, the "delivery ready days" would again come down to "2 days". Hence, we would place another order. But, after that, suppose there is no shipping for the next two days. Then, the "delivery ready days" would remain the same. The straight line expanding sideways represents this. Then, we would receive the '3 days stock' ordered two days back. Thus, the stock would shoot up to '5 days stock'.

But there is no need to worry about. In this method, the amount of stock cannot exceed the '5 days stock'. This is the reason that we don't place any order until the "delivery ready days" comes under or touches the lead time. When no shipment as expected, stock increases up only up to sum of the 'amount of stock' and the 'lead time' stock! This is the extreme situation that we may encounter!

Let's see the graph furthermore. The "delivery ready days" increases to 5 days stock at the eighth day. But at the eleventh day, the stock decreases to 2 days and we place another order. Shipping remains smooth and 2 days later, there is replenishment of the stock. This process repeats. This is the basic mechanism of "proper timing and proper quantity ordering system."

9. How can we respond to any sudden and unexpected demand?

It is difficult to respond to the breaking demand during the period of lead time.

Suppose we place an order with a farmer for direct delivery to avoid any chance of stock-out. We calculate the timing of ordering by using the number of days required as 'lead time'. By the way, what would happen if an unexpected thing happened during the period of the lead time? Let's see the stock of rice at home as an example. The stock status of rice in a certain family of four members was as follows:

(Unit: meal)

Date	1Thu	2Fri	3Sat	4Sun	5Mon	6Tue	7Wed	8Thu
Rice of stock (meals)	84	72	60	48	36	24	12	0
Consumption of relatives				20				
The revised stock				28	16	4	-8	-20
		Order						Delivery

Fig. 54: Day-wise stock of rice in a family

Amount of rice necessary for one day: 3 meals a day * 4 persons = 12 meals

Lead time to arrange rice from the farmer: one week

As the lead time is one week, the amount of the stock should be "3 meals * 4 persons * 7 days = 84 meals." Well, as we expect the stock of rice to be exhausted by one week, we place an order to the farmer on one Thursday. In the normal course, there is a regular consumption of the rice. The rice stock trend will be like as shown in Fig. 54. We expect the stock to become zero is on the eighth night. We expect to receive new consignment of rice ordered on Thursday last in the daytime or the evening of the day. Then, there should not be any problem. There would not be any risk in uninterrupted availability of the rice in the chest. In other words, there would not be any waiting or suffering due to no stock. By the way, what about if there is sudden arrival of ten relatives on

Date	1Thu	2Fri	3Sat	4Sun	5Mon	6Tue	7Wed	8Thu
Rice of stock (meals)	84	72	60	48	36	24	12	0
	Order							Delivery

Fig. 55: Changes in stock pattern on arrival of some guests

Sunday? It is natural that we need to treat them with lunch and dinner. The speed of consumption of rice in such a case gets accelerated in an unexpected manner. What would happen in the stock position? Let's refer Fig. 55. On the 6th night, there will be only 4 meals left. So, on the 7th day, some persons are likely to suffer from want of rice. It is the situation of 'stock-out'.

Thus, there may be an occasional hike in demand during the period of lead time. If we do not take suitable measures, then there will be an incidence of stock-out. But it is very difficult to take a countermeasure during the period of the lead time. This is even though there is some sign of the upcoming situation of stock-out. The arrival of "Unexpected Guests", in this case, causes an upset in the demand during such period.

There is a need to have "safety stock" to prevent any incidence of stock-out.

It is important to prevent any stock-out during the period of the lead time. Then, the idea that immediately comes to mind is jacking up of the stock. It is possible to make provision for maintaining the stock at a higher level. The level is such that there is an allowance to respond to any special circumstances. Such special situations are like when the demand exceeds the expectation. We call such a special provision in stock keeping as "Safety Stock". This is a very well-known terminology in the science of stock control. In the case of the family mentioned before, it is possible to take care of by having another 2 days stock of rice. Also, it should be kept in another storage facility (Rice chest). This is the jacked-up allowance.

2 days stock is equal to "3 meals * 4 persons * 2 days = 24

meals."

Usually, nobody minds having such an allowance while carrying out daily operations. The safety stock is like emergency provisions. We should use it in need only when the demand swings upward during the period of the lead time. Due to the unexpected guests, on the 6th night they have only 4 meals stock and on 7th, the stock of rice runs out. Then, we can use this safety stock. If we add 24 meals (safety stock) to the stock of 7th, the amount of stock of both 7th as well as of 8th night would turn positive. Thus, it becomes quite easy to cover the necessary amount. We can avoid any crisis due to stock out!

(Unit: meal)

Date	1Thu	2Fri	3Sat	4Sun	5Mon	6Tue	7Wed	8Thu
Rice of stock (meals)	84	72	60	48	36	24	12	0
Consumption of relatives				20				
The revised stock				28	16	4	-8	-20
Safety stock							24	
The stock including the safety stock							16	4
	Order							Delivery

Fig. 56: Safety stock helps in overcoming
any sudden increase in demand

There is an index called "Service Rate" that decides the amount of safety stock.

The formula to work out the safety stock is as per the following formula (using statistics):

Safety stock = safety coefficient * standard deviation * √(lead time)

"Safety coefficient" depends on the information of 'how much stock-out we can allow. If we decide to keep the stock-out rate at less than 2%, the service rate becomes 98%. "Standard deviation" is a Statistical term. This is a measure of the deviation or variation in the number of daily shipments. It is a bit difficult to calculate by a pocket calculator, but it is very easy using a PC. When the daily shipment is steady, the standard deviation becomes small. As a result, the amount of safety stock would also be small. Likewise, there may be a situation when the daily shipment fluctuates a lot. In such a case, the standard deviation would be larger. So, the amount of safety stock would also increase as per statistical calculation. Refer Fig. 57 to check typical trend of safety stocks under varied conditions!

How to decide the safety stock

2% possibility unable to correspond based upon the past tendency

	Service rate	95%	98%	99.90%	99.98%
Amount of the safety stock	Commodity A of stable demand	18 Pcs	22 Pcs	32 Pcs	37 Pcs
	Commodity B of unstable demand	103 Pcs	129 Pcs	192 Pcs	218 Pcs

※ The average shipment is 50 pcs in either of A and B.

Fig. 57: Typical safety stock under varied conditions of service rates and standard deviation of the amount received

10. How to respond to a known future trend by use of an "Index"?

Use of a "Seasonal Index" is common to take care of seasonal variation in demand. There are some goods for which the demand rate changes by the season. For example, there is often a special demand of some commodities in early spring. It slumps as summer approaches. This cycle repeats every year. Thus, there are cases when we know the change of demand beforehand. It is possible in such cases to leave the matter of working out 'stock' norm to the automatic calculation. We should do such a calculation for the inventory control by using a predefined "Index". Suppose a certain wholesaler is handling some stuff for school. Its demand increases in the spring. Until March, the shipment per day was about 20 pieces. But in April, the wholesaler expects it to increase to about 80 pcs (as shown in the table below).

	Jan	Feb	Mar	Apr	May
Average shipment per day of the month	20	17	22	80	20
Accumulated average shipment	22.8	22.2	22.2	27.0	26.5
Index				4	
Necessary Amount	22.8	22.2	22.2	88.8	26.5

Fig. 58: Use of Index to take care known surge in demand

Let's recall the ordering system already introduced earlier. As per that, the process is to calculate the necessary amount on the basis of actual data of the past. Thus, we may prepare only 20 pieces for the month, April. Then, the stock-out would happen. But it is possible to make use of an index (of 4) in such a situation. We multiply the accumulation average shipment by it (4) in April. This is so as that is the demand expansion period. The necessary amount per day becomes 88.8, and thus, it is possible to avoid any incidence of stock-out. In May, when the demand returns back to the normal pattern, we can resort to the original operation. This means, during the month with normal demand pattern, we can omit the use of this index.

We should use "Life Cycle Index", if we need to sell out all the goods in a short time.

There are some commodities that are in use for a short time only in a certain season or so. For example, a particular item may be in demand in the summer only or in other words, a "Summer Limited Commodity". For such a case, there is a need to set up a target different from the usual stock control to take care of this. The basic aim in this case is to have no stock left out "at the end of the selling activity". The stock control is unnecessary if we sell in a short time the entire amount of a commodity. This is more so when we might have bought the commodity in bulk at a cheaper price. There is a clear logic to buy or produce an extra amount of the commodity in such a case. Yet, we can think of having the stock control using an index called the 'Life-Cycle Index'.

There is a need to have a couple of information for setting

this index. One is the quantity of planned sales. This is, "how many we expect to sell out during the given sales period". Other important information is the actual data of past performance of the commodity. It can even be on the basis of a commodity that seems to have a similar tendency of sale.

Let's assume that a similar sales tendency will be available from the past sales data. Then, based on this, there can be a forecast about when and how many we can sell. This would be the planned sales amount. There may be an initial turning on and initial replenishment schedule as per this. When sales start, we should compare the forecast with the results. We should correct the figures of the expectation until the end of sales period as per this. We can examine the effectiveness of such an index by the following classifications:

[Note: "Undulation" is the amount of the stock increases and decreases in a repeated manner. This occurs like the wave in a cyclic order. The index correspondence is effective for the repeating change like season of ② below. About ③ and ④, the artificial correspondence is inevitable.]

① Usual undulation:

This is to correspond with the safety stock calculated by lead time and the average of shipping.

② Seasonal undulation:

This is to correspond with the seasonal index based on the

data of the past.

③ Event:

This is to correspond with the prior information captured. It is common to capture such data in cooperation of the marketing division. The data is about how much they want to sell and how.

④ Man-made undulation:

This is to reduce it by appropriate evaluation and close communication system. Such communication is between production / procurement people and the distribution people.

Lessons the translators have got from Chapter3

1. Managers should know that they can do the stock control by controlling "Inflows".

2. Managers should check whether the current ordering method is the best or not. They should be brave enough to challenge existing practice and go for a new ordering method.

Chapter 4

Warehouse and organization that improves the power of stock.

1. "Seiri" and "Seiton" to the stock

The warehouse on which company has spent a lot of money may not be in a state of a "Good warehouse". It is quite difficult to find a "Good warehouse". We may see a photograph showing rows of splendid shelves and boxes in an orderly manner. It may look like a good warehouse in a sparkling building. But there may be bad movement of stock in such a warehouse. Then, it is natural that we cannot call such a warehouse as a good warehouse.

By the way, let's now take a refrigerator as an example of a warehouse. We can consider it is not managed well when there is "withered-green" like situation of goods inside it. We may also observe that there is difficulty in putting or picking up something. It often occurs due to poor storage and handling of goods. After experiencing such situation, it would be easier to imagine if a warehouse is good or not.

There are only the necessary things in an expert's warehouse.

Here, let's see how a well-managed refrigerator and its surrounding may look like. This happens when an expert person with knowledge of stock control maintains it. Around the refrigerator, there would be no obstruction to opening or closing of the door. On opening the door, there would be no goods inside packed like sardines. The inside look would be very refreshing and well-illuminated. We may find the fridge filled no more than 80%. It should be possible to see everything inside without removing any item. There may be some foodstuffs marked "For sale" by a seal on it. It becomes quite clear that these are the foods with a long shelf life. These are often bought in bulk when they were cheap.

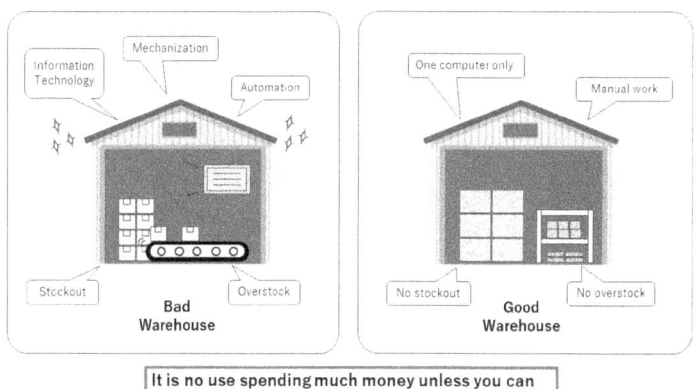

Fig. 59: Investments made in a warehouse: Good or bad!

We would find Fresh vegetables stored in an orderly manner in the vegetable room. Also, we may find this room not completely filled with vegetables as a matter of healthy practice. In such a fridge, it is quite usual to find everything inside it in a tidy, neat and clean as well as fresh condition. The refrigerator or warehouse maintained by an expert has a good circulation of goods as shown in Fig. 60. Such a person goes for purchasing of necessary things only as a matter of habit.

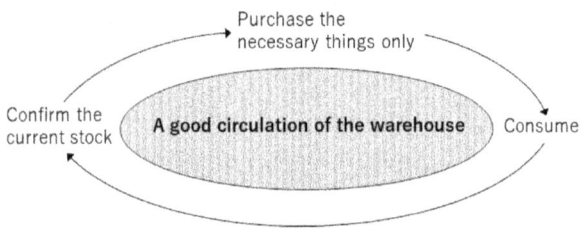

Fig.60: Characteristics of a good warehouse

To create a warehouse where there are no invisible places!

The first step to achieve stock control is to avoid having any invisible places. An expert person has clear knowledge of what and where various commodities are. It is quite common that the content of a refrigerator often changes its locations. So, a mechanism needs to be there in place to know anytime what and where things are there. There is a method in which we should decide the location of each item. Basic idea is to know anytime what and where the goods are there.

For instance, it may be like the following:

a) Location of beer is at the right of middle step,

b) Snack is at the lower step,

c) Daily dishes are at the middle step, and

d) Homemade pickles are at the right of the middle step of the fridge.

This is an example on how to define the place for each item for storing in a refrigerator! This makes it possible to recognize at a glance if the stock of beer is running out. Also, it would be possible to avoid any stock-out at ease. There would hardly be any time to search for locations where to store the fresh purchases.

It is important to share the rules of operation of a warehouse with everyone.

Suppose it is a case of a refrigerator of a person who is living alone. In such a case, even if there is no clear decision about what and where things are there, it may not matter so much. It is quite natural that the refrigerator may not be so big! Above all, the person to put stuffs in it and the person to take out these from the refrigerator is the same. But, in case of a refrigerator used by all members of a family, a single individual doesn't put the stuffs in and takes out. In such a case, there might be possible to have many problems. These are like:

a) Moving the stuffs without permission,

b) Buying unscheduled things, or

c) Consuming the food meant for visitors by some member of the family.

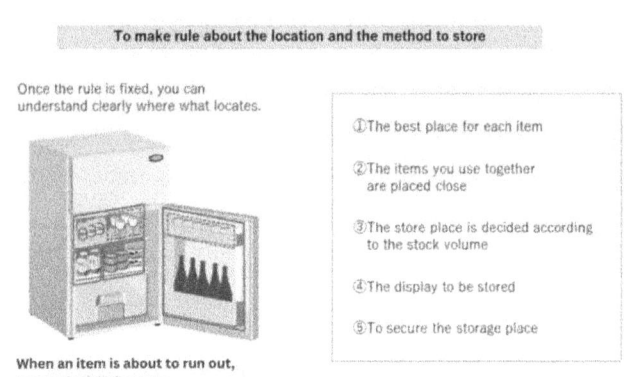

Fig. 61: Rules can make life simpler

It is important to observe certain rules for effective operation of any warehouse. This is true even for a refrigerator used by a family! For example, typical rules may be like:

a) "You must not use any item located here (at a particular place)", or

b) "You must follow the rule of first in first out" etc.

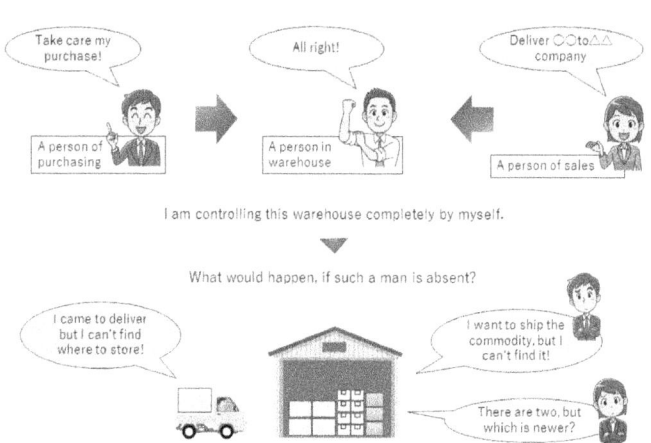

Fig. 62: Situation of a warehouse when controlled by a single person

It is a fact that most of the people who like others to follow rules, they don't often take interest in making such rules. Also, they hardly put in efforts to make any mechanism so that it becomes easy for the people to observe rules! They also don't try to make people knowledgeable about the rules. Thus, they don't enforce strict observance of it. This is even when there are some regulations already defined! This point is very important.

Let us take an example of a refrigerator that stores drinks in a convenience store. Suppose it is important that one should take out drinks only from the front side. There would be no instruction to the customer like, "Please take the older one". It is quite understandable. But the storage system is such that the customer would buy the older one anyway.

But there may be a case where an old and experienced

storekeeper manages a warehouse. He does everything relying upon the memory about receipt and shipping of goods from it. In such a case, this person is the rule himself or herself. Apart from this, it is another matter how such a person may be thinking. In such a warehouse, when the person concerned is absent, there may be a lot of disturbance in operation. Suppose this warehouse keeper becomes sick for several days. Then, goods received in the warehouse in the meanwhile may be lying here and there. It is possible that there may be piling up of some goods at the entrance of the warehouse. This may occur if the operating person didn't know the prescribed storage locations. It is because nobody other than the warehouse keeper has any understanding about it. Also, there might be a need to make a shipment of some commodities by any means. Due to the difficulty of searching, there might be a need to deploy a lot of staff to search out the stock. The root cause of such poor state is quite clear in this case. It is, "There are rules, but nobody has shared the same among the operating personnel". So, it is important to make a system such that everyone understands the rules in the warehouse. This would make it possible to have low-cost management.

There is a need to apply the idea of "5S" for stock control.

The most wasteful work in the warehouse is "spending a lot of time searching out the necessary stock". The effort put in to search anything which doesn't exist at all is the worst waste of all. We must have a warehouse that everyone involved understands. Otherwise, such kind of worst situations might occur quite often. Let me introduce "5S" as a concrete method that may come handy to better manage a warehouse. 5S makes it easy for everyone to have a clear understanding of any warehouse. "5S" is well known all over the world now-a-days. This is being used for improving production sites in all kinds of factories. 5S is five words whose initials are all "S" in Japanese language. The concept of 5S may become very clear by going through Fig. 63 below. Let's try to apply it in the case of a refrigerator as an example for training.

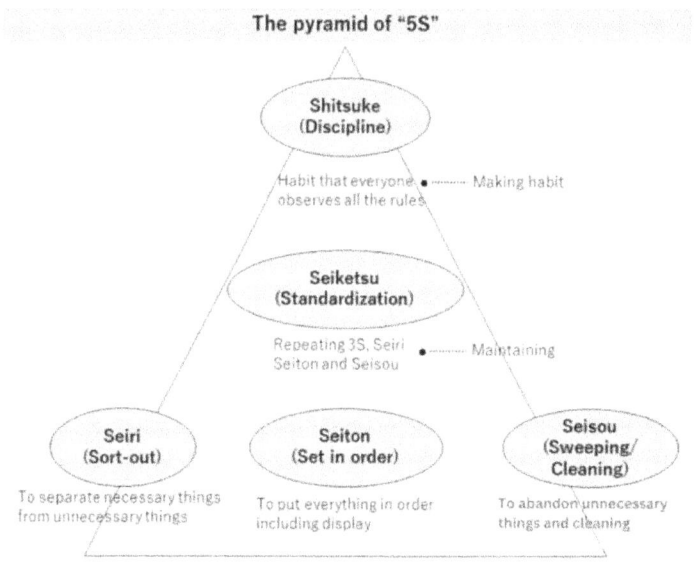

Fig. 63: 5S Model

A fridge should contain only the necessary things. This is possible by executing the system of stock control. Basic idea is that a warehouse should contain goods to meet the present requirements. In such a case, we can expect the refrigerator to be very neat inside. The first step of management is to understand 'what are things available at the moment'. For this, there is a need to practice "5S" activities at a regular basis. Otherwise, it is impossible to understand at any time what are the stock available. In short, we can say "5S" is the basic for stock control. Its importance is the same both for a refrigerator as well as a warehouse!

Everyone around the world calls the system as "5S". But as a matter of fact, there is only "3S" which are actual actions. These are, "Seiri" (Sorting)," Seiton" (Setting in order) and "Seisou" (Sweeping / Cleaning). "Seiketsu" (Maintaining cleanliness) is to repeat above three actions (i.e. 3S) on a continuous basis. Basic purpose of this is to build a habit or discipline in the due course. "Shitsuke" is a situation when everyone observes activities of "3S" without asking. Everyone does so almost like a reflex action. This is like acquiring a habit or "Discipline."

The pyramid shown in Fig. 63 expresses the meaning of 5S as mentioned before. Then, let's begin with doing "Seiri" (Sorting out) of the refrigerator. In this, we should separate out unnecessary things from necessary things. Then, we should throw away the unnecessary ones.

Culture of sorting out and disposing off unnecessary things is an investment.

When working on stock control, the hurdle of this "Seiri" might be the highest. It is because there is a need to throw away the unnecessary things. This is like a psychological barrier. This arises as a company has already paid money to get these things. But we must understand that having stock means 'paying of a large sum of invisible cost'. We should not limit this thinking only in case of our refrigerator. It is also applicable to our bookshelves and our storeroom. We may find something in our room because the storeroom doesn't have space to accommodate. This is a symptom that it would be an object of the examination to sort out. The invisible cost here is about "space" and "time". We may think about the answer in our own way by going through the following questions:

a. How much space are we using to store our stock?

b. Without having some particular stock, would we be able to put more necessary things at the place?

c. If we don't have some stock, would we be able to use the place in some other way?

It is wasteful if we cannot use our precious place in more meaningful way. There may be something that we may not need anymore. But it may be lying occupying valuable space. Let's reflect once more on the possible problems due to the stock we have. To execute "sorting out" requires an exceptional courage.

a. No matter how good we keep the things in a systematic way order, it gets cluttered soon.

b. We come often to search for something.

c. It takes time to search for something.

d. Often, we can't find a thing even after a long search.

e. We found the same item after returning from shopping of the same.

By now, I hope we have a clear understanding on how we waste space and time more often than not. Finally, we are able to realize that we are using money in a wasteful manner. There is a need that the management should have a positive mindset. They should put in a lot of brave efforts for Seiri. Then only, they can make operations better by discarding the unnecessary things. Such actions may lead to unlock a lot of money. A company can invest such money for a better future. This also helps in freeing up of valuable space for better use.

The first is the arrival of a commodity, the first should be the shipment by the principle of "First-In First-Out".

It is natural that we do not like to throw away any stock as far as possible. This is because we have acquired these with great pain. The mechanism of "First-In First-Out" is very useful as well as effective to avoid such a situation. It is a technique for keeping the freshness of stock. In this, we ship those commodities first that we received first in the past.

Let's adopt the mechanism of "First-In First-Out" in our refrigerator. There may be some items for which we would always like to have some stock in the refrigerator. We need to buy these items from time to time due to their regular consumption. We do such buying of fresh stocks while there are still some old stocks to avoid any stock-out. At this point, it is important to distinguish the old ones from the new ones. We should arrange its positioning such that we can use the old ones first. The mechanism to ensure this is quite easy. There is only one door in our refrigerator at home. It is always the front side from where we take out our goods first. So, we need to put the old ones at the front-most portions.

There is a method to put things in the refrigerator to avoid any trouble during use.

There is an important point that while putting the stuffs inside the refrigerator. This is, we should try to make it easier to take out the necessary things for use. When we receive new or fresh ones, it is desirable to move the old ones to the front side and keep the new ones at the back side. We may feel that it is troublesome to do the arrangement of new and old stocks like this. Thus, we may leave the old ones as it is without separating from the new receipts. In such a case, the old ones would stay for a longer time. In the end, these may need abandonment due to aging and deterioration of quality. Moreover, every time before use, there could be to a lot of wastage of time. This is due to the need for confirming the validity date of each foodstuff. But it is possible to avoid such wasteful exercise altogether. This is by practicing "First-In First-Out" as a rule.

A typical rule could be: "Keep the old ones in front and the new ones at the back side". When it is impossible, there may be a different rule. This could be like, "Keep the old ones at the right and the new ones at the left". Of course, this would depend upon the size of storage space and shape of the stuffs. When we fix any such rule, it is important that everyone should understand it and be able to follow. Additionally, we can use some kind of signage also. This is like a display of a caution note: "Use from the right side!". Such a display can prevent anybody from forgetting the rule due to any carelessness.

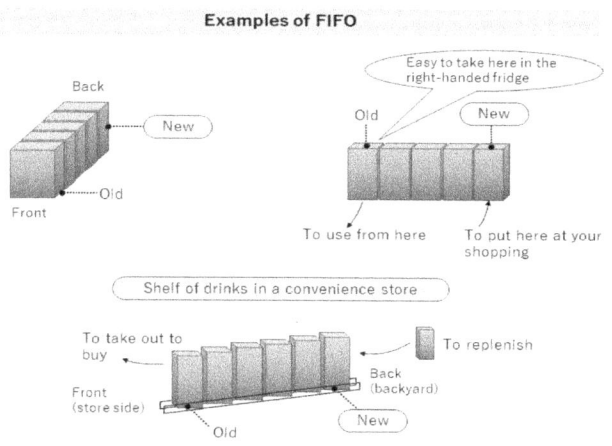

Fig. 64: Various mechanisms of "First-in First-out"

2. There is a need to devise a mechanism for 'how to store the stock'.

To create an image of the ideal storage

An easy-to-use warehouse is the one in which each stock is there in its ideal location. To create an image of such an ideal storage system, it is very useful to draw a plan first.

Again, let's try this concept in the case of a refrigerator. An ideal state means, even by taking a glance into the refrigerator, we can learn about the reality. To reset all items, it is better to prepare a plan first using a big piece of paper. It is better to write down the points that are usually forgotten. This way, it would be easier to keep goods in the refrigerator in a planned manner.

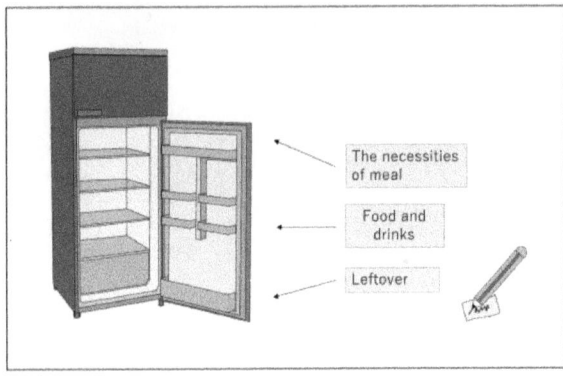

Fig. 65: Outline of a refrigerator for drawing up a storage plan

It is important to draw a sketch of the refrigerator on a sheet of paper in detail. This should include an internal view of the shelves also. This is like a precondition of making appropriate arrangements of the storage space. Once the sketch is ready, it is important to write down on the paper about every item location-wise in the fridge. It is convenient to change the place when there are bold tags for identification. There may be suitable division of the entire space to accommodate all types of the stock as shown in the Table 7. This way, it would possible to decide with sound logic for allocating the place to store each item.

Once the blueprint of location is ready, we should take out all the contents of the fridge as the first step. Then, we should put them back again according to the blueprint. What we should not forget is to inform all the users about the rule on how to store various stuffs. This knowledge should be there among all the family members who may use the refrigerator. Otherwise, the refrigerator would soon become far from the blueprint in reality.

Division	Place	Effect
Mainly for child	Place at such a location that even child can reach easily	The child can easily take out, and his or her work is decreased.
The food for adult's drink	Place where child's hand doesn't reach	The child can't take out even by mistake.
The one that is used in every meal	To help collect items in a lot, place these so that these can be easily taken out	We can take out several necessary items at one operation by putting such items together at a common location.
The food spoils quickly such as leftovers and items with short validity period	To keep at easily noticeable place so that it attracts attention even unconsciously	The risk of getting such items rotten decreases as these would come to notice easily.

Table 7: Typical guidelines for making a plan for storage

Being reasonable makes it easy to maintain the situation.

If we arrange a fridge according to the blueprint, it attains an easy-to-use situation. This means, it becomes very "easy to take out" and "easy to store" things. It is because there is an appropriate logic to store various kinds of things. The logic is about what and where to keep things inside the fridge.

The expert management of a refrigerator is different. A normal person usually comes back from shopping and makes space to store things. He or she may be doing so in ad hoc manner. This means, the places or locations of commodities are different on different occasions! But an expert person does it in a much different way. In such a case there is a fixed and logical location to store each item. Thus, storage locations for different things are clear even before opening the refrigerator. There is no need to think even what and where we should store different things. Only thing is that there is a need to remove an item already existed in the fridge first. After that, one should keep the same item along with the fresh receipts at its decided place. This makes work very speedy. After completion of the storage process like this, it attains a state of "easy to take out" anything. This happens in an automatic manner in such process. Also, it doesn't turn into a bad situation once this kind of good circulation of goods starts.

In the warehouse of a company, things are a bit different. In this, the movement of goods might be not easy like the refrigerator when set by an ordinary person. But first of all, it is most critical to try to draw an ideal "blueprint of the stock depository". Then, it would be possible to improve if needed and check whether the improvement is effective or not. If the improvement is not effective, then, we have only to correct it. Once we have achieved a good and easy circulation of goods, we can have a feel about the level of comfort of the work. Thus, there could be a great sense of achievement as well as joy.

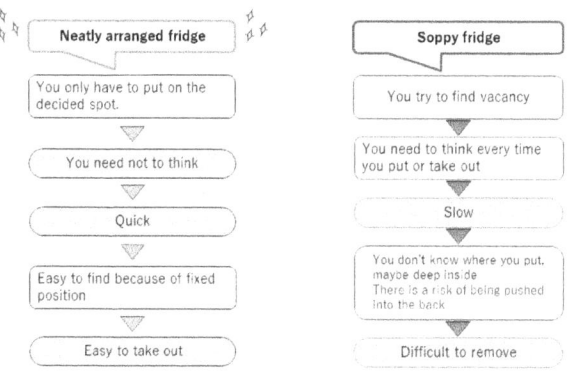

Fig. 66: Advantages of a neatly arranged fridge

To think about how to store according to the size of the place and the usage frequency

We call the method of deciding the locations of goods at some fixed places as "Fixed location" storage. If we adopt the method of "Fixed location", there is no need to change the location of various stocks every day. But it is, as a matter of fact, not a "Complete Fixation." Better use of space for storage is possible by changing locations. Such changes may be according to the change in the demand. Demand of some items may change by the change of seasons etc. To clarify the point, let us take the case of the "Beer depository" in the refrigerator. Consumption pattern of beer might be different in summer and winter. It takes wider space for storage in summer due to higher level of consumption. But we may need much narrower space in winter. So, we can use the remaining space in winter for some other item of which demand increases in winter. It is a knack that leads to change of location of any given item if its demand changes. Idea is to create space to store other necessary things in a comfortable manner.

It is quite the same in case of a warehouse. Location with wider space is necessary for storage of a large amount of a particular kind of goods. At the same time, such a wide space is not needed for goods with a small amount of stock. In other words, the size of storage space should be according to the amount of stock.

Moreover, "Frequency of the shipment" is also another important factor. Deciding on the storage locations of goods is much dependent on this. We should store the goods that we need to ship more often at the place nearer to the shipping location. It would make the whole work of shipping easier as well as speedy. For this, the technique of the ABC analysis may come very handy. I have introduced this concept in chapter 2. Please refer pages 90 to 93 for the sale amount of goods. But the cost of work is going to be the same if the work involves the same activities. It is immaterial whether it is the goods of 100,000 yen or the goods of 100 yen in the distribution centre. This is why I have used "ABC analysis by the shipment frequency" here.

Let us assume that we are discussing here about the goods belonging to category "A". These are the commodities that get shipped most often at the centre. The work efficiency worsens if we store such goods at a distant place from shipping yard. At the same time, we should not store the goods in and around the gateway. This is to prevent any suffocation of material flow in the line. Otherwise, material movement would become longer. It is preferable to change the storage location if demand of some goods changes. We should store the goods that are most often shipped at the locations from where the shipping will be easy.

The location of stock is its address.

We can make work fast and correct by providing an appropriate environment. It is where any worker in the warehouse, even a fresh worker, can work without any confusion. For this, it is important to provide the address to each of the storage locations. Such addresses are like the ones we display in front of our houses. We call such house identification as our home address. Likewise, we may have the identification number for palette station, shelf and row of the rack. Then, even for a new person it would be easy to understand the location of anything in the warehouse. A typical example of 'How to provide address for easy working at a warehouse' is as shown in Fig. 67.

The address of place to store the stock on the palette is also fixed to avoid any confusion. It is common to call such identification as "Location number". The way of controlling is to register these numbers in the store ledger of the computer. This helps in providing operating instructions to the operators engaged in the warehouse. Operators are responsible for receiving and shipping goods. Shipping work can be much efficient by following this method. This is because it makes it possible to decide the shortest routes for the shipment work. As a matter of fact, it is usual to mention such traffic routes in the printed shipment instructions.

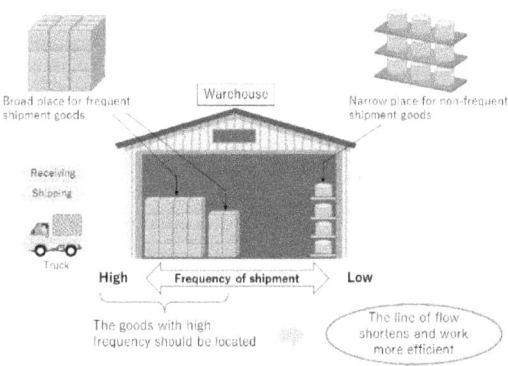

Fig. 67: Typical markings of locations at a warehouse

It might be inflexible if the locations are "Fixed".

The fixed location has an advantage that the place of any commodity is easy to remember. But it has a disadvantage too as the system of storage becomes inflexible. The size of shelf prepared for the goods in such a case doesn't change. This is even if there is a change in amount of a particular kind of stocks. Such changes may occur due to the change in the demand. Demand may change due to various reasons. The reason may be change of season or other factors. So, there might be a need to secure an extra stock area when the fixed location cannot accommodate the stock. Moreover, there may be situation when the demand decreases. In such a case, some part of the locations may remain vacant and still we cannot store other goods there. It is also quite common that there is introduction of new products time to time in any organization. This makes the situation further difficult. In such a case, only way to manage is by preparing shelves for the new commodities. To overcome such problems, there are companies that give priority to storage efficiency. They adopt a method called the "Free location" method instead of "Fixed Location".

We can put anything anywhere in the free location system.

"Free location" is a method in which we have freedom to store anything anywhere. It is suitable for the company whose commodities often change. Such a company always may be wanting to improve the storage efficiency anyway. For example, Amazon is a huge mail order enterprise. The company deals in books and various other commodities. This is why it has adopted 'Free location' system.

But, in this method, it may become impossible to manage the warehouse. This is unless we can understand in real time "What, where and how much stock" we have at any given moment. The big question is: "What would make us understand these details?" Of course, a computer can come handy. It is, thus, indispensable that we allot the location numbers beforehand. Then only we should go for executing the free location system.

Method of receiving and shipping of goods in 'free location' system

In the free location system, we can access the warehouse by

use of a computer at any time. It is possible to connect the warehouse by portable terminals. When any commodity arrives at the warehouse, the worker stores it in any shelf that he may find empty. This is the simplest way. Then, he scans the bar code of the goods using his portable terminal and pastes the same to the location. Then, he registers some kind of information in the warehouse management system. The information is like, "Ten boxes of 20 ballpoint pen are there in the location number of AA-BB-CC." But, in this way, there may be a lot of disadvantages:

a) The storage locations may become too disorder,

b) It may be necessary to go around several places to pick up the same goods for shipping.

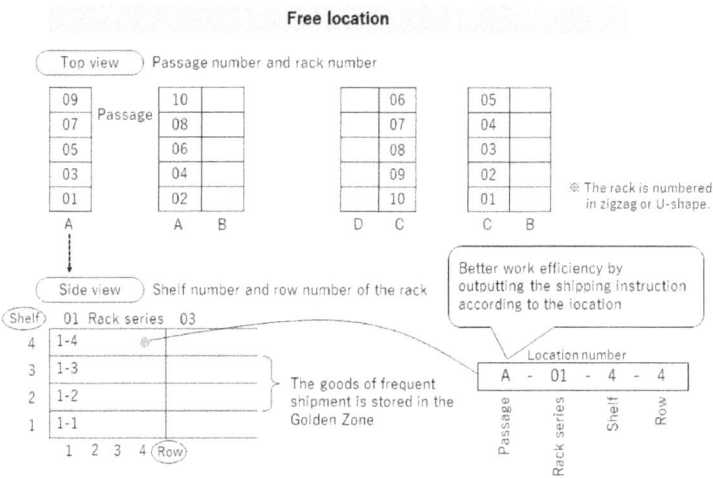

Fig. 68: Free Location Storage System

But it is possible to avoid such a situation. When goods arrive, as a first step, we should access the warehouse management system. Then, we can seek its recommendation for the best stock location. Whenever there is a need to ship goods, we can have the instruction from portable terminal. As per the location shown by the computer terminal, the worker goes to the place. He, then, scans the bar code of the location. There is information about the shipping quantity. So, he collects only the required quantity and scans the same. The computer has the information about validity and lot sizes. So, we expect it to instruct to ship from the older sequence.

In the case of 'Fixed location,' we cannot put any other goods even if there is empty space. But there is freedom to use any vacant space in 'Free location' storage system. It is possible to issue suitable instruction using the system to the stores operator. This makes it possible for him to have the shortest traffic line as well as improved work efficiency.

It is possible to achieve "Storage efficiency" and "Work efficiency" at the same time.

It would not be wrong if we say that piling of the stock up to the ceiling is not desirable. Also, narrowing the passage as much as possible is not an ideal situation. These are not the ways to give priority to "Storage efficiency" of the warehouse. Also, "Work efficiency" worsens if we pile up the stocks up to the ceiling. This is especially so when there are frequent arrivals and shipments of goods.

We may need wider space to keep the stock of the same amount if we use lesser height of the shelf. Stocking up to lower height makes the work in the warehouse easy and quick. In this, the effort required for taking out or putting in something becomes lesser. Hence, the system becomes more efficient. But it may take more time to move around the passage to reach the place where goods are there in the warehouse. As a result, the work efficiency may still deteriorate. Then, there is a method of dividing "Place for the shipment" and "Place for storing". This may help in overcoming the above kinds of problems.

Possible solution of the two problems is by the double transaction.

"Transaction" means the flow of processing in a business for a certain purpose. When we achieve two purposes at the same time, we call it a double transaction in a business operation. "Double transaction" at the distribution centre means achievement of the following two purposes:

a. Efficient storage, and

b. Efficient shipment.

To realize this, we should separate the shipping work area from storage / warehousing area. "Shipment work area" is the space to accommodate stocks for the least requirements. For example, we should limit the stock in this area to 3 days at most. As the necessary things remain available in a small area, it is possible to work in an efficient manner. Any reduction in the stock should be replenishment of the same from the main "Storing area". It is common to make such replenishment in unit of a case or a palette. If the stock of "Storing area" decreases, order is then placed for fresh supplies. The purpose of the "Shipment work area" is to make the shipping operation easy and smooth. Often, there is use of shelves. It is important to keep the width of the passage wider. This makes it easy for movement of trolleys and material handling equipment. There must be efforts to avoid any wasteful movement in the warehouse. Thus, it is better to arrange the shipment work area nearer to the gateway of the distribution centre. The unit of the operation is "No. of Pieces" or "No. of Cases". We should adopt "Fixed location" storage more in pursuit of the work efficiency.

The "Storing area" generally gives priority to the storing efficiency. The unit of operation here also becomes "Case (box)" or "Palette". This area is far larger than the shipment work area. The free location system is more adopted for pursuing higher storing efficiency.

The double transaction is a special mechanism. In this, we try to use both the good points of 'fixed location' and 'free location' storage system. It is exactly like killing two birds with one stone.

3. To understand psychology of the person who operates the warehouse

The problem usually starts from "Bulk buying" of the purchasing division.

About people who are related to the stock, the lower the level of the stock control of the company, the more lack of unity in way of their thinking or feeling. The Stores person may start getting more directions from various sections. It is not easy to convince such people by saying, "The correct stock control is to keep it at a lower level like this". It is difficult to convince such persons only by the theory. Then, let's think about what feelings may be there among the people handling the stock.

Here is a fictitious company. It is a wholesale store. Key persons related to this store are the following three people:

   a. Person-in-charge of purchasing: Mr. A

   b. Person-in-charge of warehouse: Mr. B

   c. Person-in-charge of sales: Mr. C

Mr. A did the bulk buying from a manufacturer. Suppose such buying is at a time when a standard article was nearing replacement. The brand name is "X of memories". Mr. A is usually pleased because of the lower "unit purchasing cost" due to bulk buying. He is generally praised by his colleagues by sharing remarks such as "Good job done!" It is common by doing so the purchasing unit cost would be cheaper. So, the general feeling may be that such bulk purchasing would benefit the company for sure, even if the discount sales are done. Hence, there may be a common belief that there would be the same amount of profit as before. Thus, Mr. A is generally satisfied with having purchased the commodities at a cheaper price. He may not show any interest in the shipping data of the brand, "X of memories". The feeling of Mr. A is like, "His job is to buy things well in a cost competitive manner. He is not responsible anymore afterwards". Well, is it good in the end? Now, we need to answer this question! After completion of the purchasing action, the role of Mr. A gets over. The item changes the hand. But, after this, various problems may start growing about the brand "X of memories". Let us see "How does it happen" from the following discussions.

The warehouse wants to ship the heavy stock as fast as possible.

Mr. B, who is in-charge of the warehouse, is in trouble because of excess stock. This is due to bulk buying of "X of memories" that does not decrease in an easy manner. He may be wanting to make some place for other goods. But excess stock of "X of memories" occupies a large area, and he hardly finds space to spare. Any bulk buying needs much more storage space than usually necessary. In such a case, the stock starts overflowing from the shelf to the passages and surrounding areas. This causes a decrease in the work efficiency when there are efforts to try to ship other goods. This is because of the disturbance for the work. The decrease of the efficiency leads to extend working hours. Thus, the cost of the warehouse goes up due to generation of the overtime work. With this, in the performance evaluation, Mr. B of warehouse may score much lower. Also, to cope up, other warehouses are often taken on rent for having extra storage space. This way the cost of running the warehouse further increases. Mr. B thinks that he should try to decrease the stock of "X of memories" in the warehouse as soon as possible. But he can hardly do anything in this respect as shipping is not in his control. He cannot play a direct role to receive orders of "X of memories" from customers. But this is the only way to decrease the stock of it. On receipt of order from the customer, there is shipment of the stock from the warehouse. For this, the person-in-charge, Mr. C of sales has to play an active part. Thus, he (Mr. C) only can help in decreasing the stock of the warehouse.

Sales personnel take hardly interest in the stock.

As for Mr. C of sale, he may not be very much eager to sell

"X of memories" so much. Performance of Mr. C depends on how much he has sold. Then, for his better evaluation, he would prefer to sell a new higher priced commodity. He may not show as much interest to sell a lower priced old commodity like "X of memories". Mr. C of sales doesn't know or doesn't even like to know "How Mr. B of the warehouse is in trouble". He may think, it is none of his business if the warehouse is so crowded. The simple reason for this is that he is not the in-charge of the distribution centre. It is the purchasing section that did the bulk buying. But the in-charge of the purchasing section (i.e., Mr. A) even may think that he has no relation to it. It is a matter of fact that he might have purchased "X of memories" in large quantities with great pains. But the concerned person (i.e., Mr. C) of sale has to put efforts to sell it. Otherwise, nothing good the company can expect in the upcoming future.

To link stock control a part of Key Performance Indicators (KPI's) of Purchasing and Sales teams!

We have observed that only Mr. B of the warehouse wants to ship "X of memories" in this wholesaler. Excess stock of this item is not a problem for the other persons in Purchasing or Sales. Hence, they don't feel that they should make efforts. As a result, they don't show any interest in finding some solution of the 'overcrowding of stock' in the warehouse. There may be a slower pace to ship "X of memories". The reason for this is that it is quite different from the list of hot selling commodities. But there is a need to put in effort to sell this commodity in a hurry before the consumer gets tired of. Otherwise, it may become "Long-term stock / Dead stock" in the warehouse.

In the first place, the manufacturer had tried to exhaust his stocks. At the same time, there might already be a drop in the sales speed of the commodity. So, it is necessary to make effort to sell out the stocks in hand as fast as possible. For this, joint support of Purchasing and Sales becomes very crucial. There is already some bulk buying in place! Well, coordinated actions are not taken in this company at all. The reason is that everyone is aiming as shown in the table in Fig. 69. Anybody would aim at working on areas as per the Performance Evaluation criteria of the company. This is quite logical. But, in such a state, only God can save such a warehouse from the present poor state!

	Aiming	Evaluation by company
Mr. A of purchasing	To reduce the purchasing unit cost	Unit cost of purchasing
Mr. B of warehouse	To reduce storage cost	Inventory carrying cost
Mr. C of sales division	To increase sales	Sales amount

As what every one is aiming is different, this gap makes "inventory"

You only have to change the evaluation system so that it hardly makes inventory

Fig. 69: Aims of individual sections that cause gap

By the way, such kind of problem may also occur in the stock control of the refrigerator at home. But nobody will buy the foodstuffs any more if the refrigerator is full of the stock. This happens out of mere common sense without needing any instruction to pass on. This becomes possible when everything in the fridge is visible on opening. In such a case, all the family members may share a common interest. It is like, "I want to eat the delicious ones, but I do not want to spend money in a wasteful manner." It is a matter of positive mindset. Due to this, the correction of any adverse situation also becomes very easy.

Top management can lead the stock control to the success.

There is a more important thing than the method for promoting stock control. "The top Management must show the intention to promote the stock control." Without this, any effort towards stock control would end in a kind of sudden death. This is like a situation we often experience in case of sudden increase in the wind speed. The root cause of "Why stock control doesn't go well" is due to the complex organization structure. Most organizations have many divisions. Such divisions are like, "Manufacturing division", "Purchasing division", "Sales division" and "Distribution division". It is quite common that all these divisions work towards their individual targets. This means, these divisions take the best actions that suit their respective divisions. It is usual to adjust any gap in their activities by adjusting the stock. With this kind of working approach, there can hardly be any decrease in the stock. It is only the top management that can make people of various divisions to see the stock control target. So, it is important to include stock control as a part of the performance evaluation criteria for all these divisions.

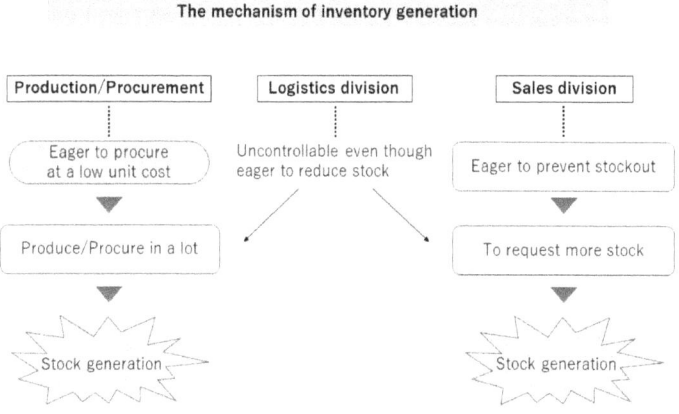

Fig. 70: The mechanism of generation of excess stock

It is possible to set a criterion of evaluation, that leads to a natural advancement of the stock control. This would lead to alignment in the behaviour of the persons according to the criterion set. Then, it becomes certain that all would work on stock control on a continuous basis. Here is an example of a company that has succeeded in the stock control by setting such criterion. The rules set were as shown below:

a. The bulk buying more than a constant ratio needs approval of the competent higher authority.

b. As for any long-term or dead stock, there would be display of the name of the concerned buyer to the public.

c. Evaluation of sales team is by final-net-sales, after accounting for goods returned.

d. Evaluation of the person-in-charge of Sales is by the marginal profit. This is upon consideration to the 'distribution' expense.

e. There is a demerit mark to the person-in-charge of Sales. This is if he does not pass on sales promotion information to the manufacturing division.

4. Bench-marking between warehouses.

To compare the abilities of several warehouses

"Bench-marking" is an efficiency improvement technique by finding and mimicking the good points. If the method is already proved to be effective, one can introduce this with confidence. We can compare the Stock control ability of each warehouse by using the following:

a) The index of "Turn-over of inventories", and

b) "ROA".

We can do bench-marking of each warehouse on the basis of

the data of:

a) The total value of the shipment, and

b) The total value of the stock in possession.

To make the comparison easy, let's calculate on some common conditions. For instance, suppose we put "Imports in warehouse A in bulk. It replenishes other warehouses at the needed time". In such a case, the result of warehouse A would be far worse for the imported commodities. This is in comparison to the other substances when we make a calculation for comparison as it is. To get a right picture, we should calculate in a specific way. This should be on the basis of "Volume of the stock corresponding to the shipment from warehouse A" only. We should exclude such commodities that the division cannot have a direct shipping. This precaution is a must when doing the calculation.

If we find a good method in one warehouse, we should apply it to other warehouses.

The difference between the warehouses becomes clear when we make suitable calculations. We should investigate asking questions like, "What is the reason that causes the difference?". Then, the cause(s) would become clear. The difference might be only due to the person "who is managing the stock of the warehouse!". It is the good news if someone is managing the stock very well. Then, the other warehouses can adopt the same method of managing.

Lessons out of Chapter 4

1. Managers should recognize that 5S is the basic for everything.

2. Managers should know the necessity to devise a mechanism for how to store the stock.

3. Managers should understand psychology of the person who is operating the stock.

Chapter 5

The warehouse and the organization that improve the inventory power

1. One should sort out the stock into three categories.

We can divide the stock into 3-categories, "Abandonment', "Reservation", and "Stock".

First of all, to reduce the amount of stock, we should divide all the stocks in 2-categories. These are the necessary ones and the unnecessary ones. In fact, for this too, we should divide the stock into three categories. These are "Abandonment", "Reservation" and "Stock".

Let's form a concrete idea of this sorting process, taking the refrigerator as an example. As the first step, we may prepare three containers according to these three divisions. Next, we should check all the stocks of a certain commodity. Then, we should put them in one of the three containers. We can divide the space within a refrigerator into different zones. These may be like, the refrigeration room, the vegetable room, and the freezer. Thus, it is worthwhile to check the commodities' temperature zone wise.

① Container of "Abandonment"

We should abandon at once anything we may find belonging to this division.

② Container of "Reservation"

This is a division in which it is difficult to decide if the commodities we can abandon. This situation happens because of a feeling that these may come in use in the future. Hence, we should adopt a practice of setting a time limit for taking a final decision on such commodities. This is like, "A date one month from now (present date)" or " A date six months from now" and so on. Setting up of such a date depends upon the commodity type, its usage, etc.

Then, one can decide to abandon it when there is no history of use of the item within the period.

③ Container of "Stock"

This contains the living stocks. There is routine use of these expected in the future (without any doubt).

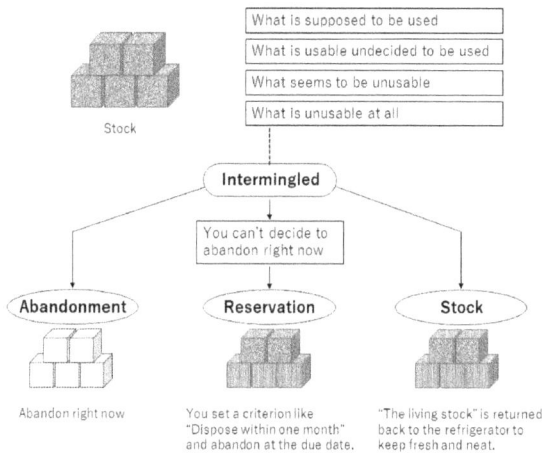

Fig. 71: Classification of stock

We should divide the stock by "the Validity" and "the significance of existence".

It is a common practice to have a standard for the disposal of goods. Such a standard helps to judge whether the stock in hand is necessary or not. It is desirable to sort out the stock according to the standard. In the absence of such a standard, it may become very difficult to carry out the sorting exercise. There should be a basic aim of making such a standard. This is to have as stock only the ones that we will use in the future in the refrigerator after sorting. We may take the validity of a commodity as an important criterion. This helps in deciding if the stock is necessary or not without any doubt. Thus, it would make the job of the division of the commodities very simple. When there is no standard available, we can begin by making a standard. Another way is to go by a system already in practice by others.

As the first step, we should check the validity of all the contents of the fridge. We should place all that are no longer valid into the container of "abandonment". There may be some commodities that are within the validity. But there may be no idea of its future use. We should put these in the container of "Abandonment". But there may be doubt about a particular commodity if it would be of use or not. We may place such item in the container of "Reservation". It may be wrong to place such commodities in the container of "Abandonment". In a nutshell, the items that we should put in the container of "Abandonment" are as follows:

a. The ones that have no validity anymore.

b. The ones whose existence is getting forgotten (Even if, there is no quality problem).

c. The ones with no possibility to use (Even if, there is no quality problem).

It is understandable that there may be hesitations in relieving any such commodities. This is so as we have acquired these in the past by paying money. But we must be able to act tough for abandoning above kinds of commodities. We must think that it is going to be an investment for the future. Here, it is important to understand the value of goods for abandonment in monetary term. The monetary value of such goods must decrease if the stock control is being practiced. This is like another index of effective stock control! We can judge the effect of such control by observing the trend of the abandonment loss over the period of time. It should show a decreasing trend.

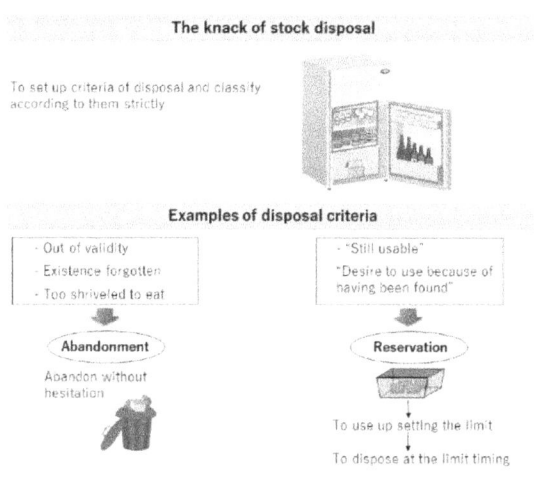

Fig. 72: Disposition of "Abandonment" stock

There may be a situation when it becomes difficult to make a decision to abandon. We may have a doubt whether we should put a particular item in the container of "Abandonment". In such a scenario, we may put it in the container of "Reservation". It is possible that we may select a lot of stocks for placing in the category of "Reservation" to start with. This may be due to no choice in the beginning. It would still a big step compared to the initial status of the stock lying mixed with the necessary and the unnecessary things.

We should do sorting in the warehouse based on data.
We can also use this sorting method for sorting the stock of the warehouse. There is no need to prepare containers, but we should try to make a similar image. The classification is the same. We should divide each of the stocked goods into any of the three categories viz. "Abandonment", "Reservation", and "Stock" based on the data.

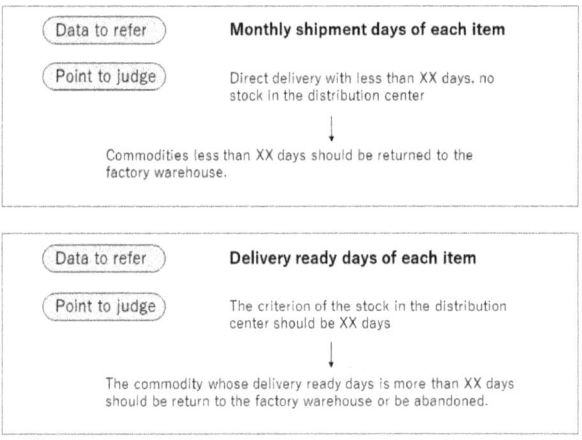

Fig. 73: Return of excess stock to factory warehouse

There may be a case that there are several warehouses of a company. These are like factory warehouses and distribution centers. Besides these classifications, there may be other categories. These are like, "Return to factory warehouse" or "Move to another distribution centre". We can put items under these heads under the category of "Reservation" as well. Now, let us try to have an image of a refrigerator or a warehouse where there are no unnecessary things. It must be appearing as fresh as the room after a thorough cleaning.

To clarify the boundary of "Reservation" and "Stock".

We have divided the stock up to now into three categories. It is common to abandon the stock classified as the "Abandonment" at once. Hence, it doesn't return to or remain in the warehouse any longer. It is also usual to arrange and store the stock classified as the "Stock" in the appropriate location. The matter of most concern should be the stock of "Reservation". We should keep the stock of "Reservation" separated from the living "Stock". We should fix some time or date by which we should take the final decision. For instance, we may fix a period like "Three months" or "Six months" from now for taking final decision. There should be a rule made to address such stocks. The basic aim should be to use up all the stock under this category within the defined period. If any stock remains at the end of this period, we need not hesitate this time to abandon. We should write the time limit of the abandonment, not the investigation date. This should be like "Dispose by the XX (date) of XX (month)" on the stock of "Reservation". Then, it is important to inform all the people involved of the meaning of this display. The meaning is that if any stock remains at the date of XX day of XX month, we are going to dispose. Since it is quite regretful, we must try to use this stock on top priority.

In the case of foodstuff lying in a refrigerator, we should treat such stock with care. We should put such stock in a transparent container with some clear instruction. Such instruction may like, "Eat by XX day of XX month" on the foodstuff. If it remains at the end of the time limit, we must not hesitate to dispose. There may be a company where the rule is to mention the value of the stock also. The idea behind such a system is to emphasize the amount that can go as waste if it remains unused. We can feel pleasant if we can use up all the stock completely ahead of the disposal time limit fixed. If we need to abandon such stock, the money we had spent would become a waste. Thus, we should keep in mind that there would be abandonment cost. We should try to get more sales and diminish throwing these as garbage. We should do this even if the profit might somewhat narrow down.

Any large disposal sale by a company is a sign to earmark the stock as "Reservation". Often, there is reduction of prices of existing products before introducing new products. Such products are personal computer and home appliance. We may find the display of a flag of "Inventory clearance" for such items. But, concept-wise, it is exactly the same. It is necessary to dispose off the "Reservation" category of stock on the top priority. But there may be an extreme situation. The product that have been sleeping in the warehouse for a long time might not attract the buyers even at a great discount. Thus, every product has a validity period in the marketplace.

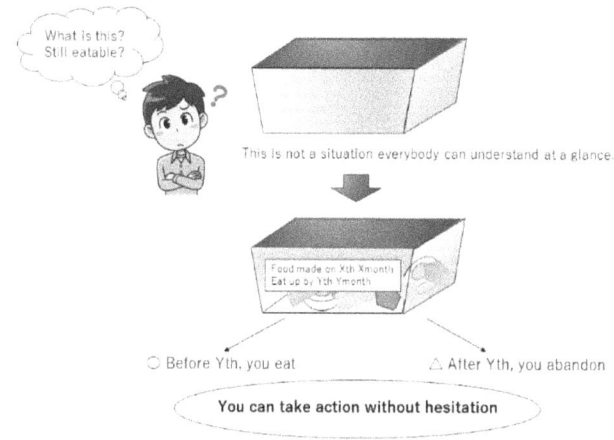

Fig. 74: Spontaneous disposal action

To visualize the "Bad stock" and decrease

As a matter of fact, we manage the stock as per certain calculations. Even then, the stock might stay for longer time due to various reasons like the change in the sales pattern. It is important to have a check on it on a regular basis and sort the stock in the warehouse. The idea behind this is to keep the stock at the least possible level. First of all, we should sort "Good stock and bad stock" and ensure its visualization. A warehouse has far more capacity than a simple household appliance like refrigerator. So, it is impossible to visualize all items in the warehouse. This is why we should make visible only what we want to or need to make visible.

For instance, it is the "Dead stock" which we would like to decrease at once. To visualize this, we should make some criteria of special identification. This may be like, for "Goods that might be lying for one year or more". We should gather all such goods at a prominent place. Idea is that it should come to the notice at a glance in the warehouse. Then, it would attract attention of the concerned staff making it easy to act on it. This is how automatic recognition of the problem would become possible. Hence, there can be a standard system of putting some "Notice" in bold.

It is important to do this at the time when we are still able to manage before the stock becomes dead. The place can attract our attention at ease due to it being a convenient location. So, it is likely that we would act on it more often. Any abnormality may attract attention even when anybody may be visiting the warehouse for a different purpose. Such a use of storage location, thus, is an emergency measure, as a matter of fact.

Company should sort the stock in its warehouses!

For control of the stock, a company needs to resort to the practice of sorting as often as possible. This is for deciding on which stock it needs to keep, and which one is necessary to dispose. There may be a company that has not yet adopted the practice of stock control until now. It is quite natural that there may not be any such sorting exercise taken up as a routine practice. In such a case, the company should begin the activity of sorting as the first step. After doing that, the company should take it forward to start the stock control.

First of all, the company should gather two kinds of data of any product. One is the shipping amount, and the other is the stock amount. It is preferable to have both the figures in monetary term. The exercise should cover all the warehouses the company may have. The combined figure is the overall stock of the product maintained by the company. Next step is to take up such calculations for each of the products. Sometimes, it may be difficult to calculate the stock of all the goods due to reasons such as incomplete data. Some products, such as 'hot-sell' goods or 'dull-sell' goods, can be chosen! It's for sure that a big difference between the items could be observed.

Let's assume that a company has taken up the sorting work for the first time. In case of a hot-sell kind of products, it may find a good figure. There may be a lot of companies that have products whose turns of stock are less than one month. This is depending on the type of products. The hot-selling products may have less than one month turns of the sales. But in case of a dull-sell type of products, the turn-over of stock may have a swollen number. Even though the stock is not so big, a bad figure (in inventory turn) often appears. This is because the selling amount is small. Refer Fig. 75 below.

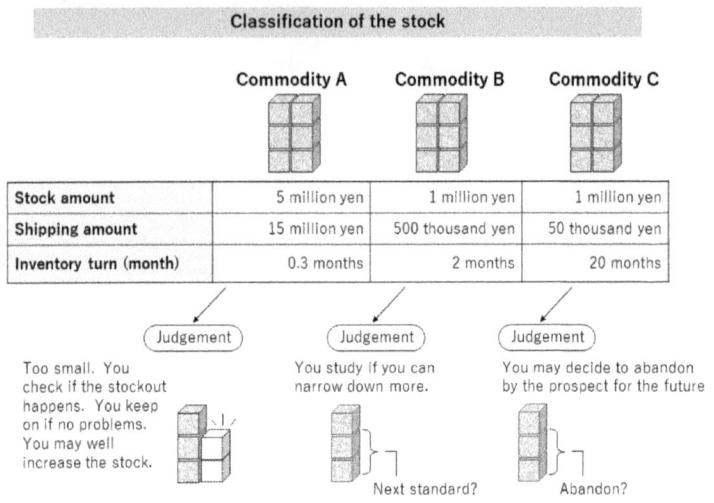

Fig.75: Relative Inventory Turns

A big difference in inventory turns is a proof that there is lack of appropriate management of stock. In such a case, it is a must to share such observation with the management for necessary reflection. Company must take a concrete step to fix a disposal standard. This should be in the terms of the inventory turn. It is like, the inventory turn must remain below a specified figure. Management of the company may need to have a little courage to decide upon the disposal standard. This is because such an exercise is generally based on some kind of assumptions. The assumption may be like, "there will not be a sale of a particular product in future" etc. The company may decide that it would dispose the product whose turn is over 6 months to begin with. Then, the management should try to observe for a while. Based on this, there should be a judgment of disposal if any item of the stock hardly moves.

One may take a chance to go out to visit the site of stock. This is with an idea of sorting the stock seeing the actual status of various goods. This is particularly important if it is difficult to capture the data of the shipment. One may consider a high amount of dust on a product as a sign that the stock has not moved for a long time. Then, there may be a note on it with mention of "Abandonment candidate" using a red label. First of all, one should concentrate on the stock that seems to stay for the time being and paste some sign on it as a first step. After a gap of several months from putting such signs, it is important to check the stock again. If the stock with the label of "Abandonment candidate" still remains as it is, one may make a clear decision to dispose of such goods.

2. The stock decreases if we exclude the constraint condition.

The upper limit of the stock depends on the constraint condition.

In a company, often management may remain satisfied deciding that there is stock of XX months. But it should check the amount of stock from the viewpoint of whether there is potential to decrease. The amount of stock may be too much! There may be a lot of opportunities if we fix the limiting condition of each item. Then, it becomes possible to check if the stock is more than the limit set. The pattern of sales and purchasing constraints are often the deciding factors. Depending on these, there must be certain fixed amount of stock of each item. Thus, the followings are generally considered as the constraint factors:

a) Restrictions on the purchasing lot sizes; and

b) The delivery frequency.

"Purchasing lot" is the size of the lot decided between the purchaser and the supplier. This means that we can buy an item in lots like 10 pieces or 1 case by unit. The "frequency of delivery" is like there is shipping of an item once or twice a week. Thus, there is a fixed number of deliveries, and this is set by the seller. These are something beyond the control on the part of logistics management.

Even if one may need only 5 pieces, one has to buy 10 pieces, the lot being 10 pieces. If the frequency is once a week, one has to keep stock for one week. If business in a day is 5 pieces and there are 5 operation-days in a week, then one has to keep 25 pieces as stock. In this case, one must have 30 pieces due to the lot size of 10 pieces.

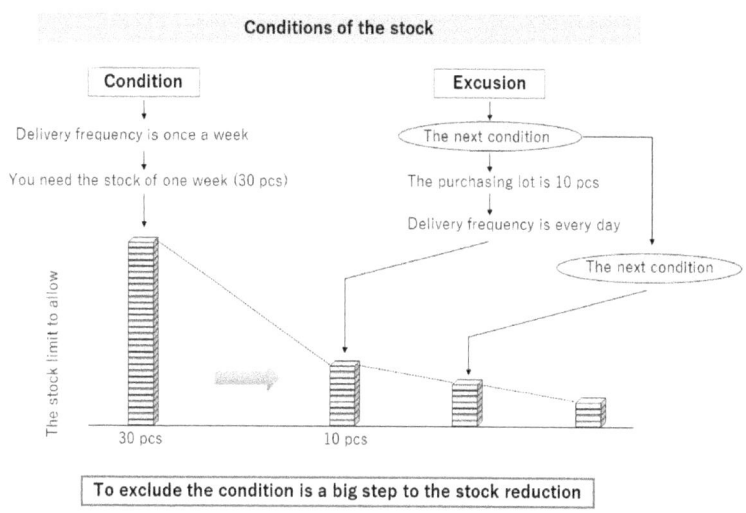

Fig. 76: Conditions of the stock and its effect

In the above-mentioned case, we may fix the limiting condition of 30 pieces. If the stock is more than 30 pieces, it is more than the limiting condition. Then, we should judge it as "Excess". In working on the stock reduction, we must be careful. We should not forget to exclude the constraint conditions. The upper limit of the stock can change if there is an increase in the delivery frequency. How many would be the upper limit of the stock become if the delivery frequency becomes every day? The answer is 10 pieces, not 5 pieces for one day. The reason: In this case, we have excluded one constraint condition (i.e., the delivery frequency). But the next constraint condition (In this case, the purchasing lot) will come on the way. Besides this, "Production lot" can also become a constraint condition. For example, there may be a condition that once production starts, it will produce in lots of 100. Thus, there will be production of at least 100 pieces.

Shortening lead time is effective in stock reduction.

Shortening of lead time also plays a significant role in the stock reduction. When the lead time is long, it is necessary to prepare the stock to meet the demand forecast for the future. But, in such a case, the probability of the "calculation becoming right" may be lesser. Thus, one needs to prepare safety stock considering any deviation of the shipment. This is to prevent the situation of stock-out even if the lead time is long. Cooperation of the supplier is also necessary to shorten the lead time. At this point, it may be important to share the effect of shortening the lead time with the supplier. There should be a check that there is no increase in the stock at the supplier end due to the reduction in the lead time. What one has to do is:

a) To shorten the lead time of the supplier, as well as

b) To manage the lead time from the customer.

The basic idea is to strike a balance.

It is necessary to proceed with the stock control based on "ten days" when the lead time is "5 days to 10 days". It is very serious if we fail to keep the promise of "ten days" at most. This is why we often decide to prevent stock-out in any case. In such a case, there is every possibility that stock will increase due to uncertainties. If we make the lead time as "5 days", then we can decrease the amount of the safety stock. This means that we now have half the period the safety stock should cover.

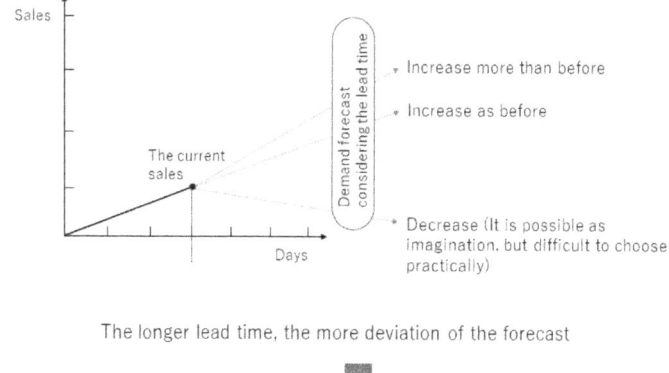

Fig. 77: Effect of demand forecast when lead time is large

To reduce the purchasing lot to reduce the stock

When the purchasing lot size is 3000 pieces, we have to buy 3000 pieces even we may need only one piece. Demand and sales may change and decrease after we have purchased some commodity. To reduce such a risk, the purchasing lot size should be as small as possible. Reduction of the lot size to the least possible level is impossible only by our own effort. Cooperation of supplier is necessary. It may be better to learn from the supplier about any effect that would be there due to reduction of the lot size. For example, the supplier may need to make up any upcoming loss by some hike in the price in such a case.

There is a pitfall in the bulk buying.

The bulk buying at a time at a cheaper price has no problem as long as consumption of the commodity is going well. But one should be careful. The situation may be like, "At present, there is no problem even if there is bulk buying". But the market conditions may change from time to time. The condition may be like, "There is a considerable decrease in the consumption rate for the item".

I found the refrigerator of my house actually in a state of break down while I was writing this book. The inside was pitch-dark when I came home and opened the refrigerator. I found the ice of the icebox was all water. I got dumbfounded in such sudden occurrence. I recalled that I thought of "Bulk buying" to refill the fridge with various foodstuffs. The risk of the bulk buying was there in such a case. I was to go shopping on the way back after my business on that day. I scheduled the bulk buying. I was going to do a bulk buying because the inside of the refrigerator was almost empty. But now feel, I was lucky because I had no time to go for shopping. If I had gone for shopping, I would have bought a lot of foodstuffs. All those would have got spoiled due to break down of the fridge. Thus, it would have been impossible to realize the advantage expected due to reduced cost in bulk buying.

The stock and the risk are opposite sides of the same coin. Bulk buying increases the risk. Demand may change. Moreover, quality of the stock may also get deteriorated due to frequent and long power cuts. It is also a fact that we cannot rule out the bulk buying in totality. But it is very important to recognize that it has an associated risk.

To get the highest effect in the constraint condition

There is an important consideration about the constraint conditions. We should have the greatest achievement by doing business under certain constraint conditions. It means that it is not possible to achieve a result beyond a certain point. This is if there is a limit in the ability of a certain section, no matter how much efforts we put in. Let's see the influence and kaizen measures that a constraint condition exerts on the whole.

Suppose a company has a system of making the shipping instruction on paper. Then, they distribute it to the workers to do the shipping work. Once there is shipping according to it, the orders on that day become complete. The basic system is that they print out the "Shipment Instructions" on paper. They prepare such instructions in the combinations according to the destinations. It may be the case that the ability of such shipping doesn't go up any further. Then, it becomes the upper limit of the shipment ability of this warehouse (or, a limiting factor).

In this company, there is a constraint. It will not be possible to start the following activities until there are "Shipment Instructions":

a) Combination work of the shipment as per shipping instruction, or

b) The shipping jobs

It may be the case that the company has taken orders for more time than the usual time of the day by some reasons. Then, the printing time gets postponed as a matter of fact. Thus, the shipping instruction papers would take time to hand over to the workers. So, the workers would be waiting for a while. It is exactly known as the "Waste of waiting" according to the Toyota Production System. This would lead to postponement of all the subsequent activities. As a result, there would be unavoidable delays in the shipments.

Constraint in such a case may be the capacity of the printer. This may restrict the entire shipping ability. In other words, the constraint condition can be the "Ability of the printer". It is quite easy to overcome such a constraint by increasing the number of the printers. But it is necessary to examine first if there is any possibility of improvement. Idea is if we can avoid any new investment. Let's think of changing the work or the process, its mode of operation and / or the sequence. We should check if the printing capacity may not influence the work in an adverse manner. This is from the point of view of waiting of workers and shipping delays.

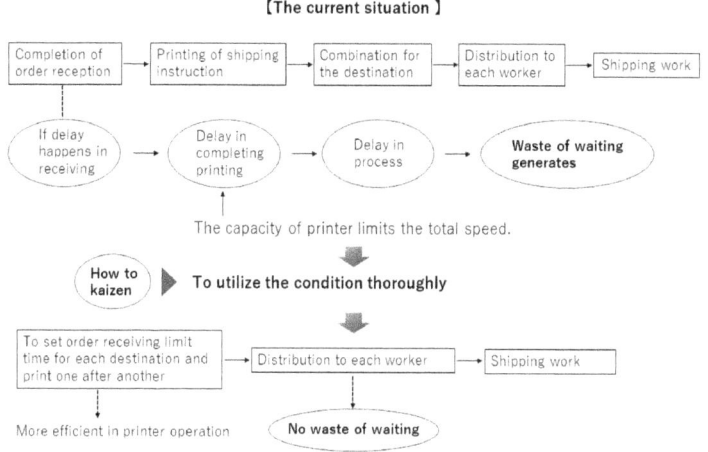

Fig. 78: An example of how to improve work to avoid waiting of workers

For instance, there is a way to go for a change in how to receive orders. It is not necessary to start printing after receiving all the orders. This is unlike the existing practice. Refer Fig. 78 to understand this well. In this, the deadline of the time to receive orders of far distant addressees is set earlier than others. The person at the reception controls this and doesn't accept any fresh order after the set time. Then, there is printing of the instruction for the shipping operation and handing over of these to the shipping workers. In this method, there may be a delay of an order somewhere. But it is possible to print for the orders of some other destinations meanwhile. Also, as a result, the printer would never remain idle. Thus, there can be improvement in the entire shipment ability by devising a new way of work. As a result, there would be no disturbance in the shipping work by the constraint condition.

There is a similar effect by the constraint condition that sometimes we face in our daily lives also. Suppose we make a plan to entertain our visitor. We prepare a course meal starting from appetizers to desserts. Let's think of situation when there is a time limit to finish. In such a scenario, we must think in a different manner. Our aim should be that the visitor enjoys the meal relishing the food served as much as possible. We should plan in such a way that the visitor finishes eating without any loss of time. To achieve this, we should adopt a strategy. We should offer various dishes according to the speed of eating a particular dish. We should not serve the next dish when the visitor is still eating the previous dish. In such a case, it would cool down before he starts eating. Those who eat together with the visitor should adjust as per the eating speed of the visitor. Otherwise, the flow would stop. Suppose eating speed is slower than that of the visitor. In such a case, the meal stagnates because of a delay in serving the next dish. Also, it is not effective even if such a person finishes eating earlier than the guest. Suppose we serve the plate early. It would still not be effective. This is because the meal would cool down for the visitor. The reason is that the visitor's eating speed remains the same. In other words, the visitor's eating speed is the constraint condition. It is possible to achieve the best effect by the cooperation of those who eat together with the visitor. The basic idea behind is that there shouldn't be any slowing down of the speed.

3. To decide up to how much to correspond by the stock

If we keep on thinking about emergency, thinking of stock control becomes difficult!

My father who was enjoying a party with some friends hit on the second party in my house. This was the result of a sudden decision. My father called me saying, "I am going to bring my colleagues at home from now, please take care!"

This caused a big upset about the stock of the refrigerator. We may even say this kind of thing as the biggest problem about the stock control. The first problem was due to the fact that such a party was not expected. It was unavoidable that this sudden change would misappropriate the stock of foodstuffs. For instance, the stock available might be enough for breakfast of the next morning. Now, there was a need to manage breakfast of next morning out of the stock meant for next day's lunch. This way, the change would lead to a cascading effect on the usage of foodstuffs afterwards. Further, it was likely that there was already a schedule to go for shopping the next day. But now, the refrigerator could be almost empty after the party. This might cause panic and would lead to go to a convenience store instead to buy foodstuffs. Foodstuffs are more expensive at convenience stores. Hence, it would cause a loss for the household economy. The second problem could be that there was now a sudden demand of unexpected visitors. In the mind, there would be an automatic thought process about such a situation in the future too. This would lead to another phenomenon in managing the stock. There would be a thinking about the correspondence to this for future! It means such a thinking would be an integral part of stock control measures thereafter. So, it becomes a problem if we don't know whether and when our father who has gone out would come back with the guests. It becomes impossible to manage the situation without having some extra stock always. This may mean carrying of some exclusive stock for the visitors as a matter of routine practice.

As a result, the amount of stock in the refrigerator would always be much higher. Another point is that there may be occasions when there would be no visitor. Then, this would leave the family with no option but to consume at times some old foodstuffs. We can summarize the influences of such sudden demand on the stock control as follows:

a. To go for emergency purchases from local convenience stores even though it is expensive.

b. It leads to extra trouble in the operation of the stock afterwards.

c. It makes it necessary to maintain / prepare some extra stock always .

To cover the sudden demand by prior notice by sales and marketing division

We can say that a sudden demand is a "Bad guy" on the stock control. But it is quite easy to root out this bad guy. A sudden demand arises when there are "unexpected" visitors. This is in the case of foodstuffs in the refrigerator discussed in above para. Stock control can be easy if we can remove the term "unexpected" from "unexpected visitors". Father tends to bring along some "visitors" home in an unexpected manner. The voice of father is the root cause of the sudden rise in demand.

Suppose the voice of the father is like, "I will bring my companions home on the coming Saturday". This makes the task of stock control of the refrigerator of the house quite easy. Indeterminate information like, "I may bring them on Saturday" is good enough. It makes a far greater difference from the situation with no prediction at all! If there is a prior notice, it becomes possible to go for shopping. It also makes it possible to think about the menu. There may be some menu according to the stock that may be available on Saturday.

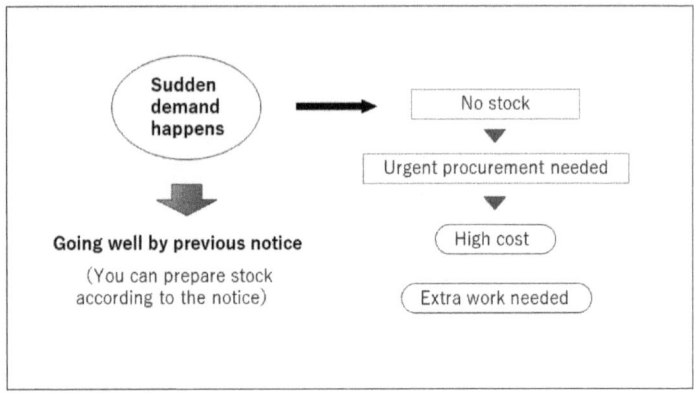

Fig. 79: Impact of sudden rise demand with and without information

The housewife might think that she should exhaust the stock as much as possible by Saturday. So, she could have a plan to go for shopping on Sunday. It might make a big fuss if there are visitors on Sunday all of a sudden. She might have to run to a local shop or order a home delivery service to treat the guests. This is because there might be inadequate stock for them. Thus, such an unscheduled act would need extra time, effort and cost.

Exactly similar problem often occurs in the world of the business too. The person or the manager who is like the "Father" is the person-in-charge of sales. He feeds the following kind of the information in the system down the line:

a) "How the business is going on at present, or

b) When and how many may have to deliver etc."

Such information influences the stock control level of the company.

4. We must be careful about decreasing the stock too much.

Insufficient stock might cause a problem.

With inadequate stock control system, it is quite tough to maintain proper stock. There are increasing number of companies that try to reduce the stock anyway. This is even though they do not have a proper stock control system. This is so because they also realize very well that too much inventory is not good. The problem of insufficient stock might happen in such companies. They narrow the volume of inventories based on their feeling alone. The feeling is that they don't want to increase the stock too much. In the process, they do not make any different treatment between the products. In the process, they sacrifice the stock of the product of "hot sell" type also. They do so rather due to lack of knowledge.

The stock of the products of hot-sell type can get sacrificed easier!

There was a company that began stock reduction by the directive of the managing director. As a result, there was decrease of the stock in a gradual manner over a period of time. But the stock-outs started happening quite often. There was an underlining cause behind such a phenomenon. This is, "The stock can get squeezed easier in case of the products of hot-sell type". It is possible that the products of hot-sell type were having a lot of stocks to start with. When the system of stock control is insufficient, stores person may choose to go in a simple and easy way. He may first think how much amount of stock they have to narrow down. There is a basic reason behind such a thinking. It is a fact that it takes much more time to gather all the required data. There was higher amount of stock for hot-sell type of goods in the beginning. This is why the amount of stock of the products of this type stood out. Thus, there was a tendency to start the stock reduction exercise from here first. Suppose there are following stocks in a warehouse:

a) 30 pcs of Product A, and b) 300 pcs of Product B.

One would first like to narrow the stock of Product B.Suppose the directive of the managing director is like, "To reduce the stock by half". Then, it is natural that one may think, "Let's narrow stock of Product B to 130 here and achieve reduction by half as a whole". Even if there is a shipment, there would be a tendency not to place order. Also, when ordering, order amount could be smaller than the earlier practice. This is with an idea to reduce the stock. But a stock-out of Product B happens. Then, there was an analysis of the trend of sale of each commodity by the data of average daily shipment. It came to knowledge that there were sales of 1 piece for Product A and 50 pcs for Product B during a given period. The stock situation was as shown in Fig.80. To begin with, the stock of Product B was only 6 days. It is a mistake to narrow down the stock seeing only the amount of the stock. One must not do it without making a comparison with the sales data.

Each stock (days)

	Commodity A	Commodity B
Before kaizen	30.0 days	6.0 days
After kaizen	30.0 days	2.6 days

Fig. 80: Change in stock pattern before and after taking action

We should have the stock that can correspond to the demand.

Even in the case of having insufficient data, we may still have to narrow down the stock. In such a case, it is very important to confirm whether the amount of the stock is appropriate or not. This is in comparison to the sales figure during the recent past. The frequency of checking of sales figures depends on the situation. It can be once a month or so. Moreover, we should consider another aspect. Some "Deviation in the demand" would always be there. The order from the customer is not going to be the same every day. Over the month, such deviation may be as high as 3 times of average orders. We may experience stock-out of Product B as a result of narrowing down the stock to the level of 2.6 days. This would be when we may receive more than 2.6 times of usual orders during the period under consideration.

We must examine in detail on the situation of past demand. Then only we should take a decision like, "How many times of the average demand" we should prepare. If there has been any recent incidence of stock-out, it is necessary to increase the level of stock. In case of Product B as mentioned above, it is likely that "We receive a 3-days order for one day". Hence, we should have at least "4-days of stock for ensuring necessary safety". Otherwise, we may not have any advantage out of "Stock reduction" in this case. We should avoid any chance of "Loss of sales" caused by the stock-out. But we must take necessary precaution while analysing the sales trend. It is important to check if such an increase in demand was artificial. The salesperson may be looking for some bargain sale.

5. From 'stock control' to 'logistics'

To match the supply activity to the market trend

We cannot expect a stock reduction only by construction of a stock control system. A proper stock is possible if actual flow of the orders is always according to the expectation. We devise the stock control system on the basis of certain assumption about the order flow. The basic system is to replenish the stock. But the reality is not so simple. For instance, there are certain conditions for a manufacturing shop. These are like, "Production plan" and "Production lot". There may be a situation to have only 100 pieces more than the regular shipping quantity. But manufacturing shop may have to produce 500 pieces more. This is due to the production lot size is pre-decided as 500 pieces.

It has been common for any manufacturing unit to attach priority to "Productivity". Productivity means "Production Efficiency". As a standard practice, production has not been caring about the data of unsold goods. They were hardly focusing on how to match the "Supply activity" to the "Market trend". There has been another area of activity called the "Logistics". It has to take care of such management.

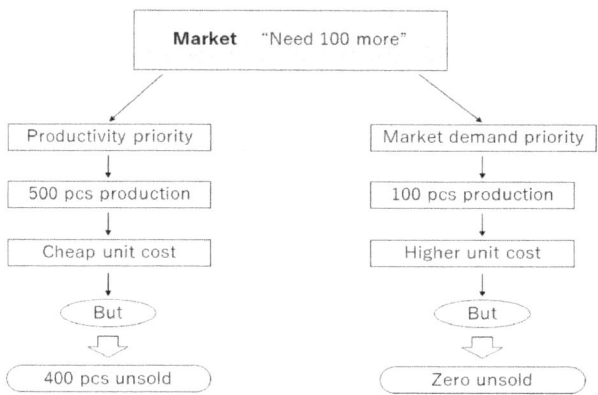

Fig. 81: Accumulation of unsold goods
when productivity is priority

Goods should never be unavailable in the market!

The word "Logistics" may be difficult to understand. Its meaning is "detailed organization and implementation of a complex operation". This is as per the dictionary. There has also been another understanding about the activity of "Logistics". It is the activity of organizing the movement, equipment and accommodation of troops. It was during the Gulf War when there was real attention to the term "Logistics". The key to win was how to supply to the far front line from mainland. It was about supply of the "Necessary things, Necessary amount and at Necessary timing". To achieve such objectives, it was important to capture data of "What, How Many and Where" there was a need. As a matter of course, another information was also critical. This was about how long it might take to transport various things to the front.

It is quite the same in the case of preparing and shipping goods in the business too. It has now become very important to capture data of "What, Where and How Much" of different goods are to ship. Then, it is important to send it according to this. Thus, "Logistics" is an area of management responsible for transporting goods. It should ensure transporting necessary goods to the front line i.e., to the market without fail.

To reduce 30% of stock by the logistics

In a certain manufacturing company, they had decreased the inventory by 30%. This was visualizing the realities of the stock situation. The company produced these stocks in-house at its factory. As a routine practice, company kept these at the distribution centre. From the distribution centre, there was shipping according to the customer order. It has been the general pattern. There was no improvement in any production facility. There was a change only in one aspect. It was to make available: a) The data of "Amount of the stock" and "Delivery ready days" of the distribution centre, and b) Sharing the same between the distribution division and the production division.

Data of shipping status from the distribution centre is a report on the actual demand. Such demand is for the real market. This information changed the method of production to a great extent. The production division started producing goods matching with the needs of the market.

Until then, the production division used to make the production plan based on the sales plan. Sales Plan was being made by the sales division. The production division used to have no information about the actual sales situation. Then, they had no other way but to use the sales plan of the sales division. This was serving as the closest information about the possible sales of goods. But, as a matter of fact, it was not corresponding to the actual sales in 100% of the cases. Sometimes they used to produce goods that were more than the actual requirements. So, it was natural that some such goods used to remain idle in the warehouse. This was because of lower sales than predicted. Also, there might be problem of lesser than required production of some goods. So, they could be on the edge of stock-out of these goods. This, in turn, could be as a result of increase in sales.

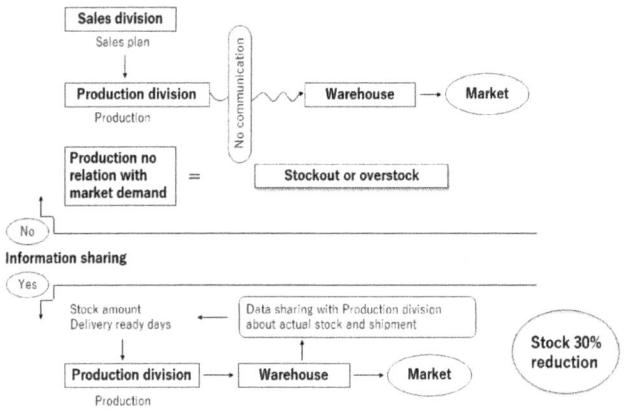

Fig. 82: Impact of information sharing between divisions

It is important to understand the following:

a) Sales situation in the market, and

b) Amount of the stock corresponding to the market.

For this, we should approach the logistics. This way, we can avoid producing any unnecessary goods. As for necessary goods, the rule is not to produce an item until the time it becomes necessary.

Lessons the translators have got from Chapter 5

1. Managers should have courage to abandon unnecessary things. This is in spite of the fact that there may be some financial loss.

2. Managers should capture the limiting condition that causes the stock.

3. Managers should be careful about decreasing the stock. They should decide the size of the stock to correspond.

Chapter 6

To reduce the stock by the supply chain

1. To reduce the stock by the supply chain

To connect from production to sales by the supply chain

From production of a product until its sale to a consumer, there is connection like a chain of work centers. In a company, such a chain starts from its manufacturing factories. It flows to the wholesale stores and further to the retail store. Thus, this chain takes care of production, shipment and distribution of its products. It is common to call this kind of linkage of streamlined supplies of goods to customers as the "Supply Chain".

It is possible to manage the stock throughout the supply chain through the contribution of each of the entities. But to be able to do so, we need to have a far higher level of stock control. It is different from the control required for a single point, entity, or company. Please refer to Fig. 83 to learn the difference clearly. It is easy to understand that by opting for a single point stock has a big advantage. In this, it becomes possible to reduce the stock furthermore.

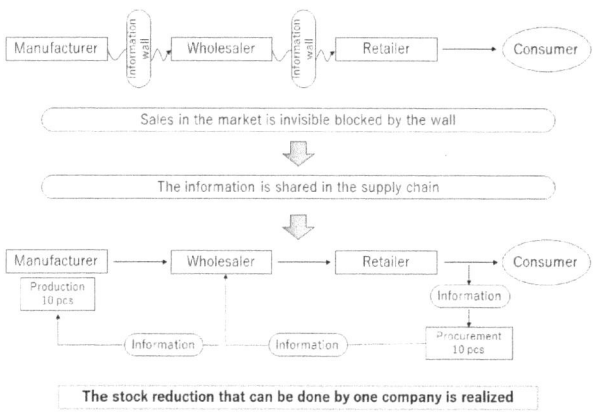

Fig. 83: Multiple stock points vs. single stock point in the supply chain

To make the best use of the sales information for stock control

Stock control is best done based on the shipping information as the starting point. For instance, the wholesaler provides the stock to the retailer. He prepares the next order for purchasing. It is for an amount that seems to be necessary from the manufacturer. He does so on the basis of the shipping information of the retailer.

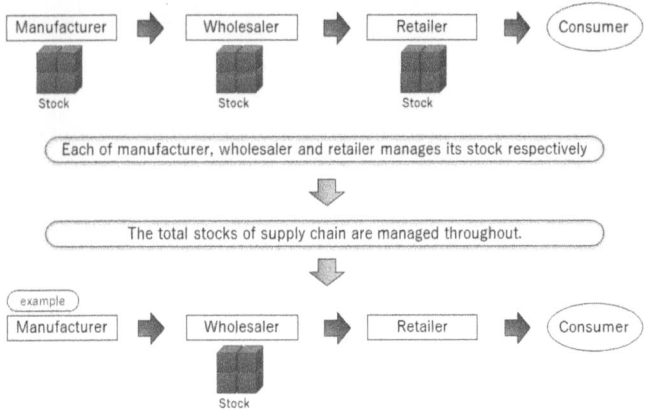

Fig. 84: Production based on real information of sales helps in reducing stock

But there may be a return of the goods once shipped as "returned goods" for some reason. The reasons could be lower sales than expected or due to some quality concerns. If there are some returned goods, the amount of the stock may increase. This is because there may be some new stock prepared already. Generally, there could be some kind of information barrier. This could be:

a) Between the manufacturer and the wholesaler, and

b) Between the wholesaler and the retailer.

The barrier is in respect of the real requirements. As a routine practice, they correspond only to the order they receive.

There are some wholesalers who buy based on the sales information from the retailer. They try to use it for stock control. They try to avoid any waste in the form of "returned goods". We call this kind of operation as POS (Point of sale) based. To put it straightaway, it is the information that a clerk records in the cash register. The retailer records it by scanning the bar code. This way, the accuracy of the stock control goes up by understanding sales at the retailer's end. This is because it reflects the real demand. Suppose there is information that the sales of a particular retailer are not good. Then, the wholesaler can judge that it is needless to prepare any more stock. It is easy for him to foresee that there may be some returned goods sooner or later.

Thus, the stock reduction advances in the entire supply chain if we can make some effort. We should be able to make a production plan in an accurate manner. This can be possible if we make such a plan based on the information of sales to the final consumer. This would cause a stock reduction at the higher level. An entity alone of a company cannot do so in an independent manner. There is a need to have management of the entire supply chain in such a case. It is common to call such management the "Supply Chain Management" or, in short, SCM. Thus, we can define SCM as the management of the flow of goods and services. It includes all processes that transform raw materials into finished products. It oversees each touch point of a company's product from initial creation to the final sale.

Order placing might disturb the achievement of SCM!

It is quite possible that SCM may not go well even if there is a correct understanding of the final demand. It is because there is an activity of placing an order. A wholesaler can't avoid delivering a product as per the order placed by the retailer. This is even though he judges based on POS information that:

a) It may not get sold at the end, and

b) There is a possibility of receiving some goods back as "returned goods".

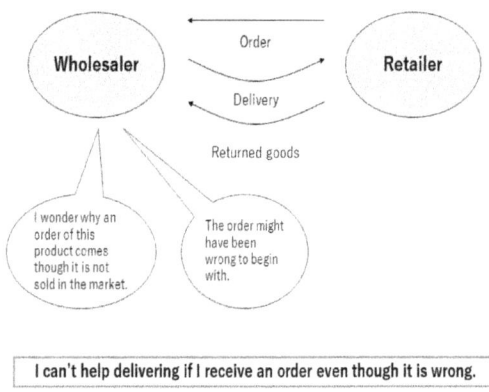

Fig. 85: Wholesaler's dilemma when a retailer places a wrong order!

The problem is that there are a lot of orders that do not reflect the real shipment situation in a correct way. We can also say that retailers are still rarely practicing stock control on a regular basis. There are a lot of cases when they place an urgent order, observing an empty shelf at the shop. In such a case, one would have no choice but to deliver goods according to the order. This is even though one might not expect the placing of an order in such a situation.

The stock more than actual demand arises due to Bullwhip Effect

There is a word known as "Bullwhip Effect". This is a typical phenomenon. It inflates the order placing at different stages. Thereby, it creates a big difference in stock control of the supply chain management. Let us understand how it happens from the following discussion.

Bullwhip is a whip with a long, heavy lash. A small shake in hand makes a large swing at the top of the whip. Such a phenomenon is called the "Bullwhip Effect". It usually occurs in supply chain management. In other words, a small move in the market gets amplified more and more, transmitting it up in the supply chain.

Let us assume that there were 3 pieces of a certain product sold by the retailer. Then, the retailer may start thinking, "Possibility of a little more quantity". Hence, he places another order of 5 pieces or so. Likewise, the wholesaler may also think, "There are a little more sales possible next time". So, he places an order of 10 pieces or so to the manufacturer. The person in charge of the manufacturer, in turn, may place an order of 15 pieces with the production division. He may be thinking in the same way that "Sales seem to be good. We have to avoid the stock-out". The production division may also like to produce 20 pieces or so. He may be thinking of the production efficiency. Fig. 86 shows this kind of Bullwhip effect in a pictorial way.

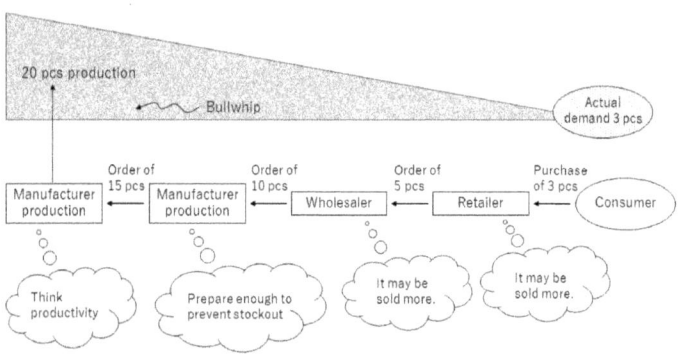

Fig. 86: The "Bullwhip Effect"-An example

So, though only 3 pieces were actually sold in the market, the information might get amplified. This is in the successive stages of the order placing from the retailer. Now, let us imagine:

"What would have been the situation if all the stages had the same sales information?"

The manufacturer would not decide to produce as many as 20 pieces in all probability. So, one way to prevent from having extra stock is that we should provide a suitable environment. It should be such that all agencies involved in the supply chain be able to see through the original demand.

There is also a method in which the supply side manages the stock of the demand side.

There is a method called VMI (Vendor Managed Inventory). In this, the supplier doesn't take the order as it is likely to be inaccurate. "Vender" here means the supplier. So, "VMI" means that the supplier manages the inventory. The VMI method is often compared to a sales model that had been followed by some Japanese merchants long time before. It had been a business model well-known and famous in Japan. This business has been run following this model for the past 500 years or so. For example, the system of selling medicines by a company called Toyama had been like the following:

A seller used to travel to visit his or her customers to provide a medicine box to each of them at their houses. The box used to contain several kinds of medicines. At that time, as a practice, the seller would not raise any request for any payment. Suppose the customer would get ill due to reasons such as a cold, or a headache. Then, he or she would use the medicines from the box provided. As a routine practice, after some time, the seller would pay a revisit to the customer. It was customary to replenish the medicines consumed by the customer. At that time, it was customary for the customer to make the payment.

We can find such a system at work between the manufacturer and its supplier of parts. The parts supplier has its own stock in the warehouse of the customer who makes the final products. At this point, the ownership remains with the parts supplier. The final product manufacturer withdraws parts from the warehouse. They do so to produce goods according to the requirements. The parts supplier always keeps an eye on whether there is any decrease in the stock in the warehouse. The part supplier does so across its entire supply network. The purpose is to replenish the parts consumed in an efficient manner. This way, it helps in preventing any stock-out.

The final product manufacturer gets a big advantage by operating on the VMI system. This is by way of stock reduction. The parts supplier also gets the advantage. This is by way of no need to receive any order from its customer i.e., the final product manufacturer. In the case of taking an order every day, one has to deliver the parts corresponding to it. This is even though there may be an inefficient situation, such as a low loading ratio of the vehicle. But there is no system for receiving any order in the VMI system. So, it is possible to make an appropriate production plan and deliver the parts. It makes it possible to operate at a lower cost.

Hence, such a system may be most convenient to the supplier.

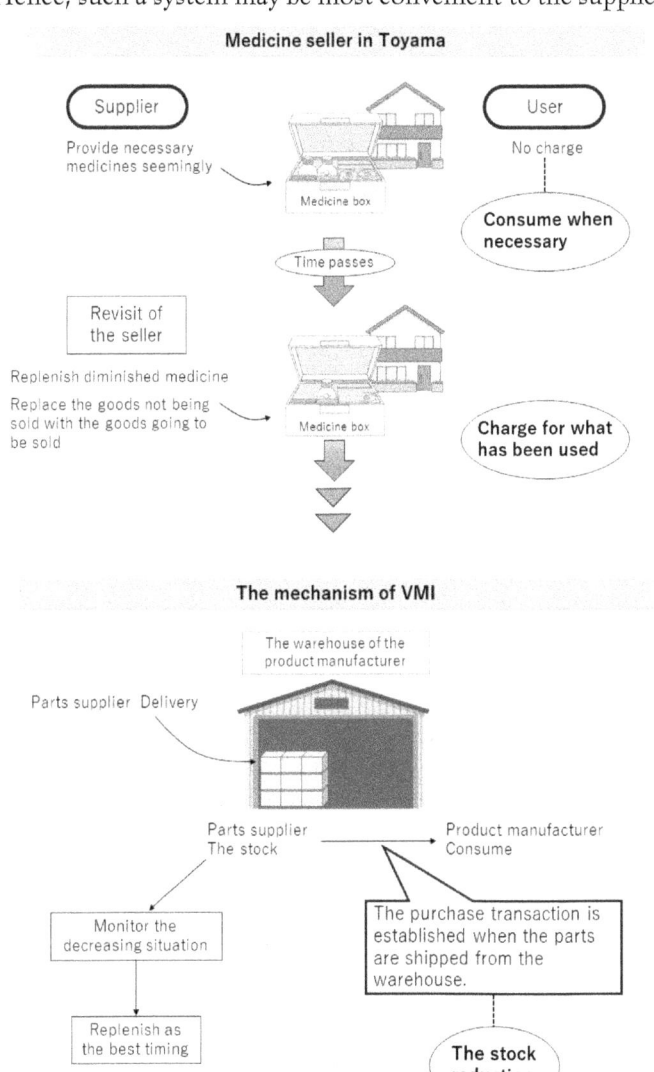

Fig. 87: Working of VMI Model

In such a case, the parts supplier may, in the beginning, perceive a disadvantage. This is in respect to the power relationship with the final product manufacturer. But, as a matter of fact, both are going to gain due to certain advantages. We call such a relationship as a relation of WIN-WIN in SCM. So, we can conclude that VMI is a method by adoption of which both companies can gain.

2. To reduce the stock by focusing on the customers, not the producers

Consumer drives the amount of stock!

Managers of many companies would often say, "The movement to reduce stock is coming in my company, too." But it doesn't seem to go well in an easy manner. To drive such a movement, first of all, it's important to learn the evil of having no stock control. Nobody generally opposes an exercise of stock reduction. Performance evaluation standard plays an important part for anybody. An individual would behave according to the evaluation standard. It's quite natural. Anybody would accord preference to this rather than acting on the call for the stock reduction. Thus, the prevailing evaluation system comes on the way in any move for stock reduction at times! So, the prevailing management system requires some kind of alignment. It should include some weight-age on stock reduction too! There are companies that still may be following the "Push type of economic activity".

In this, there is production based upon the logic and convenience of the manufacturing division. Companies, then, try to push their products to the market where the consumer may exist. But, of late, the necessity to adopt the "Pull type of economic activity" has become a critical factor. Thus, this has become a feature of the management of many companies. It has a lot of associated advantages. The pull system is to produce what the company has already sold. It is the consumer who pulls. This is a method to produce what the consumer has bought. Thus, the power of the consumers has now become the driving factor. It is beyond the traditional system of deciding on what to produce. In such a system, the manufacturing division or the supplier used to decide at their own.

From "To sell what the company has produced" to "To produce what the company has sold"

It is not the age when we can sell whatever we produce. We are likely to face a lot of trouble having accumulated unsold stock. This is particularly so if we continue the traditional mass production system. It is very crucial to reduce the losses due to the stock of such unsold goods as much as possible. For this, we must aim at a production system in which we produce only what we have sold in reality. The "Kanban system" of the Toyota Production System comes in very handy in this regard. It is a mechanism of following the pull system. First of all, there is an elaborate exercise of analysis of the sales situation in the market. This analysis is very important to start with the pull system. It is the foundation to arrive at a decision on "How much or how many a manufacturing unit needs to produce". The decision on the quantity of production for each model is according to the data of "the vehicle sold". Companies like Toyota do not make a production plan to make a large number of cars of the same model. Priority, in such a case, is not to keep the number of change-over as less as possible. The top priority is the sales situation in the market. The production efficiency comes next. Thus, the company makes the production plan according to the prevailing sales trend. This ensures that they are going to sell the vehicles produced as per such a plan almost for surety. This is as long as the tendency of the market continues.

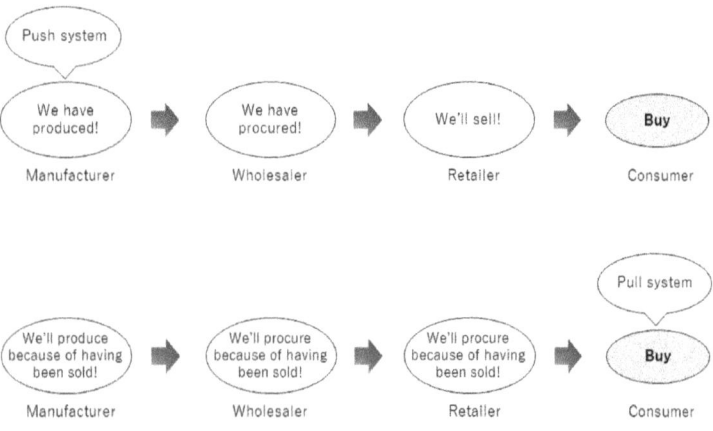

Fig. 88: Push System vs. Pull System of Production

3. How much can we reduce the stock by adopting the Pull-type Production System?

There is no waste if we replenish only what we have sold.

The pull system is not only between the market and the factory. We can extend the pull system to the supply side also. Then, we can reduce the waste furthermore. The Kanban system of Toyota evolved to help have a pull type parts supply system. In this, the factory becomes the market or the customer to the part supplier. Here, the system is to withdraw parts from the supplier, avoiding any waste.

In a vehicle assembly plant, a body flows out to the working position on the assembly conveyor. Then, a worker installs and assembles parts onto it. After this, the body is then taken to the following process. There is a system of attaching a Kanban to the parts stocked at the sides of the production line. Let's assume that this part is a door mirror. Normal practice is to deliver the parts in a box of 10 pieces or 20 pieces. When there is a picking up of one piece, the system is to take this as "used (sold)". Then, there is the removal of the Kanban from the box. After this, the system is to return the removed Kanban to the parts supplier. The parts supplier receives the Kanban. The supplier understands that there is consumption of the parts. Hence, it starts the activity to replenish the same. We must note that it is a replenishment of the same type and size of the door mirror that got consumed. Then, the supplier prepares and delivers immediately before the customer needs it.

Narrow down the stock in the supply chain.

From above, we get the idea of narrowing down the total stock in the supply chain to the lowest possible level. Here, the supply chain means "parts supplier to finished car manufacturer". The Kanban contains all details, e.g. quantity as well as the specification of each product. Kanban does the same function as an "Order receipt sheet from Toyota" for the parts supplier. The supplier can, in turn, use it as a "Production instruction sheet". Thus, in factories run by the Kanban system, there is the practice of the pull-type production system. It replenishes the amount that has already been used. Toyota follows this mechanism in a thorough manner. It produces without waste, and thus, has always been able to maintain a high rate of profit. It is a mechanism based on a clear conviction that the production, according to the sales trend of the market, leads to a higher profit rate. As a matter of course, a lot of former processes also get aligned by the adoption of this system in a gradual manner.

4. Supply chain management is evolving as a function of the warehouse

The manufacturer can deliver without receiving any order from the wholesaler!

There is an example of this practice. A food maker has been delivering goods to its wholesaler without receiving an order. The food maker plays a major role in carrying out the business. The other stakeholder of this system, the wholesaler, is its main customer. The food maker receives every day the information of shipment. It also receives the data on the inventory of its own products. For this, it uses EDI (Electronic Data Interchange). It analyses this information and data. It, then, delivers products so that there is no stock-out at the wholesaler's end. Before the adoption of this system, the food maker had been practicing a general method. It used to deliver goods every day according to the order from the wholesaler. In that method, there was a problem. The wholesaler used to face situations of 'stock-out' and 'surplus stock' at times. In that system, the order was not based on the needs of the marketplace. The food maker might be producing at times unnecessary products. This was due to the wrong information.

A big advantage in changing over to EDI system is 'not to receive any order from the wholesaler'. In this, there is no delivery of item that is out of the shipping data, or, if an order is different from the analysis. By going for EDI system, the manufacturer achieves the following:

a) Reduction in the volume of inventories, as well as

b) Reduction in the distribution cost.

Also, on the other side, the wholesaler gains:

a) By way of the reduction of ordering work,

b) Lesser efforts in ensuring proper storage and handling of inventories, and

c) Avoidance of any possibility of stock-out.

To prevent any stock-out from happening by arranging the stock on the shelves of the shop by the wholesaler!

By now, we have come quite close to the realization of SCM. This is through:

a) Understanding the needs of the market, and

b) Transferring correct information to the supply side.

It is important that the retailer should place a correct order. For this, first of all, it is necessary to provide an environment. There should be information on the number of vendible commodities already available. Suppose there are only 5 pieces of a particular commodity on the shelf of the shop. This may be even though there is a possible sale of 10 pieces in a day. An ordinary staff cannot but order only 5 pieces to replenish. But suppose there are stock of 15 pieces of the same commodity on the shelf. There is a sale of 10 pieces out of this. In such a case, the staff member can place an order of 10 pieces.

It is getting more difficult to manage stock in the shop, matching the sales. This is because new products are also coming out one after another. But we must provide for the shelves of the shop in a proper way. It is important to ensure the availability of stock of each commodity. Such stocks must match with market demand rate. Otherwise, it is not possible to place orders according to the actual sales. There may be some wholesalers who ensure their services to the retailer. Their idea is to provide for the most preferable amount of stock on the shelves. They do so by keeping in mind the characteristics of the retailer. As a matter of fact, the retailers should take initiative for such action. But the wholesalers try to provide such a service to increase the total sales. Thus, they aim at achieving a WIN-WIN relation with the retailers.

Lessons the translators have got from Chapter 6

1. Managers should know that an effective reduction of the inventory is very important. This is possible by the adoption of the pull system throughout the SCM.

2. Managers should know that they have to proceed with the exercise of reducing the stock. In doing so, they must keep in mind the customer's expectations.

Afterword

Mr. Shunsuke Tsuda has been very passionate to promote Toyota Production System (TPS). He was very serious about how to disseminate knowledge on this complex but most useful subject. According to him, there were very limited resource materials available in the English language. So, he thought of bringing out some text-book like literature on this subject. I was quite excited to work along-side Mr. Tsuda on a book on TPS and got the same published on August, 2022. It was first of the series of books Mr. Tsuda had thought of. Work on this book was the second in the series. According to Mr. Tsuda there was an excellent book in the field of inventory management. The book was in Japanese. But the book had immense potential to serve the business world. Hence, we undertook this project of translation of this book into English. This book covers the 'A to Z' of the subject in a very vivid and clear manner! Thanks to the original author, Toshiko Shibata. I am confident that the readers would find this book very useful. They may find answers to almost every kind of query in managing Inventory. The book has captured the following with a lot of simple examples to make it lively and easy to grasp:

1. The book makes it clear about the concepts behind:

    a) 'Why to keep inventory?',
    b) 'How does it rise, and it goes almost unnoticed',
    c) The mechanism of inventory control and its effect on business performance, and
    d) The risks involved when there is excessive inventory.

2. The book also makes it clear about the following:

    a) Why doesn't the 'Logistics division give birth to stock?
    b) How stock-out happens even when there is excess inventory, and
    c) How important is the synchronous functioning of procurement/production and sales.

3. The book also provides crucial guidance on:

    a) Concept of costs and expenses due to inventory build-up,
    b) Its impact on various financial statements, and
    c) How top management can make use of the data to further business mission.

4. There is a necessary clarity on:

   a) How to classify stock on a scientific basis,
   b) How to sort various commodities and collect data for easy visualization,
   c) How to interpret the real status of stock by use of three measurement indices,
   d) How to decide on safety stock,
   e) Role of purchasing in respect of 'when and how much to order',
   f) EOQ system and its limitation, and
   g) How to store for ease of handling by deploying the 5S concept and FIFO rule.

5. Last but not least, the book shows the ways and means to reduce stock across the supply chain. It explains the importance of deploying an effective inventory control system by:

   a) Making use of Sales information,
   b) Deploying a Pull System of production that focuses on customer satisfaction,
   c) Effective material distribution system (Visual Control through Kanban), and
   d) Timely action on bad stock.

There is another interesting aspect that this book brings out. It explains how inventory control leads to higher motivation of the operating personnel. Thus, doing scientific control, in turn, means increased operational efficiency! I now leave it to its valued readers for making the most use of it and share their valuable comments. There could be some inadvertent mistakes in the presentation of various concepts. Readers may please excuse us considering the real purpose behind this work. Should it serve the intended purpose, it would be our pleasure and a source of inspiration!

Samir K. Manna
Co-translator
New Delhi
India
November, 2024
+91-9990653927

www.ingramcontent.com/pod-product-compliance
Lightning Source LLC
LaVergne TN
LVHW061541070526
838199LV00077B/6860